NO MORE CRUMBS

An Empowerment Manual for the Divine Feminine

by Jen McCarty

It had come to pass that she had seen all the suffering in the world and came into depths of matter to assist.

And he came to help her.

And she is the redeemer.

You cannot get to Christ without going through Sophia.

Book Front Page Cover Artist: Emily Irena Kenyon

First Print Edition 21/07/21

ISBN-13: 978-1-956503-24-1 print edition
ISBN-13: 978-1-956503-25-8 ebook edition

Waterside Productions

Waterside Productions
2055 Oxford Ave.
Cardiff, CA 92007

Disclaimer Notice:

All of the information that I share has been received directly through my own access to the Akashic Records. Nothing that I share is regurgitated information; it is all based on downloads that I have personally received. It is so important that as you are reading these words, you exercise your own discernment and only take on as truth that which resonates for you as truth. If something does not feel true to you, then that is correct; so please do honour that.

Regardless of where you are on your spiritual path, whether you be a beginner or a seasoned explorer into the deepest mysteries of existence, the words in this book will awaken memories in you that have long been sleeping - memories of your true and abiding divinity.

The words are organised in such a way that it can be likened to light language and light codes. These words transcend the boundaries of time and space and align immediately with your heart's consciousness. The key to Christ Consciousness is through the heart.

Love Jen xx

Dedication

I dedicate this book to Liam McGenity who left us too early…. Truly one of the most beautiful souls I have ever met in my life and the man who proved without a shadow of a doubt that I really am a goddess…....

You live inside my heart now and I carry your vibration with me forever.

Until we meet again.

NO MORE CRUMBS
An Empowerment Manual For The Divine Feminine

BOOK REVIEWS

From the opening paragraph I felt held and lifted, an expansion of my heart and activity in my third eye. Part of me was shouting yes! I remember and the words flowed into my consciousness, being and belong there. As I read on, I recognised the truth of your words and the patterns of my relationships and here was guidance to co-create the reality of my desire. The wisdom shared illuminated a reinterpretation of events and a deeper understanding of who I, we are. This book is a compass for all feminines' to step into their power and navigate their lives. Thank you is insufficient for such an amazing gift of guidance.

Namaste, Karen

I have read the first five chapters of your amazing book "No More Crumbs" and I was flabbergasted at how much this book resonated with my healing journey. After I had read the chapters I experienced many activations and synchronicities start to manifest in my life. I was able to capture all of the red flags I have overlooked due to the conditioning and programming. I immediately stopped tolerating standoffish behaviour from men. I started to manifest getting a new tribe of nice, fun and genuine people to hang out with. I even got two interviews for two jobs which I had recently applied for. I am so humbled at this opportunity you have given me Jen. it will be an honour to buy and read the whole book and apply it to my life.

Lisseth Vazquez Venlo

TWIN FLAMES AND THE EVENT

BOOK REVIEWS

After a lifelong struggle of working to overcome the effects of extreme abuse in my childhood, I have arrived at perhaps the most challenging period of my life, facing PTSD, flashback after flashback, and just so much pain. I write this now because I want to say that this book, TWIN FLAMES AND THE EVENT, has come to me in the midst of this processing. I didn't know if I could even concentrate on the book, each line, or each word. But guidance said, "Read, even just one sentence for now." So I did! As I read, starting from the very first word of the prologue, I felt hope coming back! I felt God within me warm my heart and fill my soul! I felt the remembrance and knowing of the truth in each line; that even in the chaos of all of this that I am experiencing, I am "the lighthouse" that I had once promised that I would be. I had felt so mired in my life circumstances (have also experienced chronic illness for 20+ years), that I had felt my faith slipping away. Yet, as I read Jen McCarty's words, "It is absolutely and purely about faith," I felt the living, loving, Divine frequencies encoded in these words! My heart embraced them and enveloped them very peacefully and lovingly! It's really quite challenging to describe the experience of reading this incredible book! Jen was not kidding when she said, "In this book, every word is specifically directed to support you to very swiftly align with the Spiritual master-avatar being that you truly are - the galactic, angelic, timeless, off-spring of eternal love." I am writing about just a small portion of these beautiful, sacred, holy gifts that are encoded energetically in each and every word! There is just so much to say about this book that I could go on for quite some time. Suffice it to say that over the past 20+ years of my spiritual journey, I have purchased countless good books, but I honestly feel that this one is superior to all of those. Jen McCarty has channeled a book like no other! Once I started my "one sentence" in which I had been guided, I did not want to stop. Not only is this book filled with ancient wisdom, it is a dynamic Divine experience. I know that I will read and re-read this many times, as I have already started my second reading. Immense gratitude, Jen McCarty! This book will change countless lives! I know it's changing mine! Transformative, Beautiful, , Relatable, Divine! What a gift!

Jill Sutter

"Twin flames and the event" is a rare gem of a book. Within minutes of reading I had received such great insight that I literally had to take time out to reassess my life. I was then able to reframe past life events in such a way that I felt enormous relief and sense of peace as I realised that everything in my life had in fact played out to perfection. After this realisation I was straight back into the book, for it is extremely compelling as there is a plethora of information. Jen McCarty writes as an authority on the subject of twin flames, which is a very hot topic at the moment. But Jen has been interested in this field since her awakening in 1995 but has waited until this time to put her knowledge into a book for the general public. For it is now perfect timing: the book was released in the first season of Aquarius after the planet's shift into the age of Aquarius at the last equinox. Thus, Jen is writing at the cutting edge of time, as it is only now that her information could be received. It is then no surprise that this is no ordinary book, for it is infused with energetic codes to trigger remembrances and awakenings. As such it is one of a kind and I cannot wait to receive Jen's next offering.

Kate Abbott

LAW OF ATTRACTION
Little Instruction Book

BOOK REVIEW

Absolutely awesome book just as you would expect from Jen She really is a beautiful being of light with a heart that desires everyone else's light to shine. Thank you Jen

Carla

PUBLISHED BY:

Acknowledgements

Writing this book has been an extremely life changing experience for me and as anyone who has written a book knows, it takes a team to create an incredible offering that will be shared with the world.

So I'd like to now acknowledge the phenomenal team that I have around me who have assisted me to bring this beautiful and delightful book to you all…

The first person I would like to acknowledge is my Assistant Zoe for her friendship, emotional support and tireless enthusiasm to serve me and assist in getting this important message out to you all.

I would like to acknowledge my Editor Gina Baksa for the phenomenal ease and flow that I have experienced working with her, and the impeccable job she has done of editing this book. I would like to thank the artist Emily for her brilliance and sensitivity at delivering the exact image that's perfect for this book

I would like to acknowledge Eddie and Dalibor who have assisted me hugely with getting the book from my computer screen into what you are now holding into your hands today.

I would also like to acknowledge my street team comprised of beautiful brothers and sisters in my community who came forward to read the book prior to its publication.

I would also like to acknowledge my son Fin for his endless support and his graciousness at having a mother who is often very consumed with serving the collective, and I would like to thank my beautiful divine mother Mary for truly showing me what unconditional love is and showing me how precious and sacred and worthy of love I am.

I would like to thank Liam who I've dedicated this book to, the person who truly and absolutely showed me that I am a goddess, and I would like to thank my twin flame my eternal divine beloved, my muse my Damon - there is no way on gods great Earth you'd be holding this book in your hands if it wasn't for him, he has inspired every word on every page….

Table of Contents

Prologue

And God spoke:

I shall create She, the beloved daughter of my heart and I shall model her on the Rose and I will make it so that the Rose is her greatest mirror, her greatest teacher, and her greatest reflection.

My sweet divine daughter, created in the perfection of your mother: the great mother goddess herself.

Each one of you will be an aspect; a fractal of the perfection of the eternal goddess that is within you and all around you.

My precious child, as you go forth into this realm of forgetfulness, many will imprint upon your innocent consciousness lies, distortions, and false beliefs around who you are.

Please take these words as a message from my heart to yours, that from this moment you are no longer under the spell of that which is known as the matrix.

Your vibration has brought you here to these powerful and sacred words, to have this important conversation: The sacred remembrance that you are She, daughter of my heart whom I have modelled on the Rose; on the perfection and exquisite beauty of the Rose.

May you quickly be able to identify the lies and projections that the matrix seeks to project upon your eternal innocence, and may you allow these words to fully penetrate the lotus of your golden heart, to fully awaken you to your true value and your true worth.

As we go on this sacred journey into full and complete remembrance that this world will not offer you the crown of your divinity. For you are a sovereign soul, which means only you have the power to take your crown out of the etheric realm and place it firmly on your sweet divine head, in remembrance that you are a self-sovereign leader who has incarnated to show others the way home.

You promised your brothers and sisters that you would hold the mantle of leadership, in remembrance of your eternal and perpetual divinity, that they may also remember the truth of their eternal being.

Introduction

There is nothing on God's earth that could have prepared me for the success of my first book Twin Flames & The Event. The feedback that I received from everyone that read it has been very difficult for me to process, as it seems the book is not a book in the normal sense of the word.

Twin Flames & The Event is a fifth-dimensional, Ascension manuscript that is deeply transforming everyone who reads it and is acting as a powerful alchemical pathway towards abiding transformation and alignment with one's God Self.

The book was so well received, it was picked up by an incredible publishing house and they've asked me to please get on with writing my second book. So here you have it: my second book, No More Crumbs – An Empowerment Manual for the Divine Feminine.

I would just like to say that I was spontaneously guided to start writing this book on the 5:5 numerological portal date (5th of May) and I was guided to write my previous book Twin Flames & The Event on the 11:11 portal date.

On the day I started writing this book, unbeknownst to me the universe had aligned for me to receive an incredibly beautiful diamond ring, which feels deeply connected symbolically to the spiritual message and vibration of this book.

I would like to devote this book to all the incredible women out there at the moment who are working diligently on themselves. Confronting and exposing their unconscious beliefs and awakening into their true and perpetual glory as eternal and divine daughters of God.

Patriarchy has had a huge effect on men and women, and patriarchal programming has sought to entirely eradicate the role of the divine feminine from sacred scripture, particularly in Western religions.

I believe that this is very much connected to the role of Mary Magdalene and Yeshua, and the truth that was hidden and removed, which held the deep knowledge that it was She who fully initiated Yeshua into his enlightenment. It was through her gnosis, via the purification of her own consciousness, that she was able to recognise the Christ Self that dwelled in him.

It was through her recognition and her purified perception that the seed of the Christed Self within him was able to transform, to become the actualised fruit of the Christed Self.

The divine feminine plays an exceptionally important role in the awakening of the divine masculine. The Bible creators sought to entirely distort and eradicate the role of the divine feminine, by replacing her with the church fathers, thus perpetuating the false illusion that it is only through the church fathers that one is able to reach God, and attain Christ consciousness.

This, of course, is the greatest distortion and illusion that has ever taken place within humanity's collective consciousness and has created generation after generation of people who have not been able to step into full embodiment and self-realisation.

This is because a huge part of the third-dimensional patriarchal programming has sought to keep everyone entrapped in false timelines of disempowerment, attached to the false belief that one has to connect with a priest or other so-called 'holy' person in order to reach God.

This, I truly believe, is the greatest illusion that we have endured as a collective consciousness, and the intention of this book is to completely eradicate this illusion at the root level.

Welcome on this journey with me. I extend an open heart to you and I reach out a hand to you now in love and sacred kinship.

In this book, I will cover many topics such as:

The reason why women have been indoctrinated to accept crumbs in their romantic relationships.

I will share ways to completely transform this mindset and come to a place of alignment with your true self-worth.

In this book, I will share with you an extremely powerful technique called the Red Circle technique, which will help you to unequivocally stand in the vibration of maintaining vigilant boundaries, particularly around your romantic relationships.

I will share a lot about the role of Mary Magdalene and her true role with regards to Yeshua's enlightenment.

I will speak about sacred sexuality and how we heal our sacred sexuality and bring it back into alignment with God's will.

I will talk about the ageing programme and how this has affected the divine feminine, and how the ageing programme is an archaic control structure that was implemented at the time of Atlantis.

I will speak in great detail about what I've been shown about the role of the divine feminine in terms of awakening the divine masculine and the role of the true divine masculine.

There are many other subject matters which I will discuss in this book, and I'm so grateful to be on this wonderful and exciting journey with you all.

CHAPTER 1

<hr>

The Event

I would like to start this book by sharing with you all a story, something that happened in my own personal life, that inspired me to write this book. Many moons ago, I was guided to go and connect with someone whom I was deeply attracted to after one of his events in London.

My spiritual team usually arranged it so that I could meet him personally. However, this time I was very strictly guided to go backstage to meet him.

I went to the backstage door at the end of his show and waited for him. Finally, he came out, and I let him know that I had bought him an exquisitely beautiful gift from India. He then became very nervous in my presence and very self-conscious and uncomfortable and then proceeded to connect with some other people who wanted to get a photograph with him.

He then went to go and get in his car, at which point I explained to him that I had actually come to personally ask him something. He responded by saying "Please can you contact my assistant about that matter." I was flabbergasted and outraged that he had referred me to his assistant instead of inviting me to contact him directly.

At that moment, I turned around and walked away, and I promised myself that I would never, ever chase after a man ever again.

At that moment, I realised fully and completely that I am the beautiful divine exquisite Rose, and it is not my job to go out chasing after a man. It is my job to be the beautiful, exquisite Rose that I am, and concentrate vigilantly on making my nectar as sweet as possible.

In that moment when I walked away from him, I felt the most powerful, "No," arise from deep within my belly. And I kept repeating "No!!!!!! No more crumbs!!!!!" From this moment on, I will never, ever accept any more crumbs from a man.

By crumbs, I am referring to lack of commitment in all its forms: a sporadic text, a random smile, or the occasional invitation to go out. In that moment, as I powerfully walked away from him, I decided in an extremely fierce way, that from that moment on the only things I would accept from a beloved are: commitment, devotion, and true recognition of me as an embodiment of the divine feminine.

This experience was so powerful. I felt myself literally rewriting my cellular imprint as I was having this powerful life-changing conversation with myself.

I promised myself that I would never, ever chase after a man ever again.

I would draw an extremely firm boundary around myself, whereby only men who came forward in recognition of me as the divine feminine would be allowed into my sacred space.

As I was walking down the rainy streets in London, I felt the energy of Kali Ma come in. I felt like she entered into my being and she took over my body and my consciousness, and I could feel her raging within me for all women who had accepted less than what they are truly worthy of.

I promised myself in that moment, that I would forever transform, and I would never chase after a man ever again. I would never, ever allow a man into my sacred space unless he came with the energy of devotion.

I explicitly remembered that chasing after the man is definitely not the role of the divine feminine.

The role of the divine masculine is to be the bee and the role of the divine feminine is to be the Rose. I realised that so much of the patriarchal programming had instilled a vibration of lack within many divine feminines that impelled us to go out searching externally for love, connection and validation when really it is our duty and our role to activate those codes within our own being.

In walking away from the man I was in love with, I experienced revelation after revelation, and I truly realised that as I stepped into this new template, I was bringing the entire feminine collective with me.

I was very angry with my beloved for treating me in this way, but it really didn't take very long for me to realise that this was indeed a soul contract that we had made, that he would trigger this revelation within me by dismissing me in the way that he did.

I understood that it was a very difficult decision that we made on a soul level, that our interaction would take place in the way it did, and I understood that from a higher-self level, it was very upsetting for him to dismiss me in that way.

But as I was walking away from him, I felt the most incredible surge of awakening and empowerment, and I knew deeply and implicitly that this was affecting much more than just me personally.

I am extremely blessed to have a large online community, and as I was experiencing this deep transformation I knew without a shadow of a doubt that these codes would be received by a vast number of women and men in my community, who would also awaken from the nightmare of accepting crumbs from partners and wannabe partners.

I have so much to share with you all. But I really wanted to open up the book by sharing this initial story about what happened to me on that fateful day and how it completely rewrote my energetic blueprint around my self-worth.

It is my deepest desire to inspire you, the reader, to fully and absolutely awaken to your true value and true worth, and to inspire you to fully let go of the false notion of running after, chasing and searching for something outside of yourself, when your primary role as the Divine Feminine is to be in blissful ecstasy with your divine Godly self, knowing that that is the centre point of magnetism within your vibrational input and output systems.

The role of the divine feminine is to stand in her enlightened glory, at one with source energy, in full remembrance of her divinity as an innocent daughter of God; a goddess of the most high.

We promised the divine masculine that we would stand in that vibrational space, and in doing so we would hold a pristine mirror up for them, encouraging them to fully remember their eternal innocence and role as an embodiment of God in physical form.

I hope this chapter has inspired you, and I hope that it has poked at some of your unconscious patterning around what you have allowed and accepted within your own reality.

Please know I very much look forward to going into much further detail around sharing my insights with you all.

CHAPTER 2

The Red Circle Technique

In the next chapter, I would like to share with you all the red circle technique.

As I was walking away from that man after that extremely highly ordained activation meeting, I felt the energy of Kali Ma enter into my being.

She entered with such power and rage, and it felt like she used me and this powerful life-changing experience as a way to communicate to all women.

All I could hear from the deepest depths of my being was: "No! No more crumbs, never again!".

With my third eye, I could see that the goddess Kali Ma had placed a red chalk in my hand, and she was directing me to draw many, many red circles around myself, repeating the words: "No more crumbs".

I could hear her loud and clear repeating in my heart consciousness the following words:

"From now on, I only allow a man into my sacred space who comes forward with the energy of recognition."

"From this moment on, I only allow a man into my sacred space who brings the energy of devotion."

"From now on, I only allow a man into my sacred space who truly and absolutely recognises me as the embodiment of the Divine Feminine and comes forward with the necessary respect and honour that I am worthy of, as the Divine Feminine."

I felt like I was rewriting codes within my subconscious mind, and communicating to all the cells in my being, to up-level to a place which they had never attained before.

I was bombarded with memories of my own ancestral lineage whereby my mother and grandmother had absolutely not stepped into their awakening and Remembrance of who they are as embodiments of the Divine Feminine.

I realised that being the 'good girl' that I am, I had unconsciously allowed their habits and patterns to infiltrate my psyche and my consciousness, and so shape my experience of reality via my belief system.

I realised that this was prevalent within almost all cultures in society. We, as women, have not been trained to own our self-worth and fully recognise our value as innocent daughters of God. At that moment, I made a promise to all my ancestors that I would set a brand-new energetic precedent in terms of absolutely and unequivocally owning my self-worth and my true value.

I decided at that moment that this would be claimed and sourced by me. And from that moment on, I would create vigilant boundaries ensuring that only those who recognised me as an embodiment of the Divine Feminine would be allowed entry into my inner sacred field.

This was a huge moment of self-actualisation and up levelling for me within my own vibrational reality, and I absolutely fully and completely aligned my consciousness with source energy.

I remembered it was my duty to take responsibility for setting the energetic imprint or template for my upcoming relationships, through activating the codes of profound remembrance of the necessity to live one's life armed with sacred boundaries.

In this huge Awakening experience, I was able to shed an unprecedented amount of ancestral and collective programming around the deeply entrenched timeline of women accepting crumbs in all areas of our lives.

At that moment, as I walked down the rainy London streets, visualising this red chalk in my hand, drawing many, many thick red circles around myself, I knew that I was entirely rewriting my blueprint as a Divine Feminine. And I knew that as I stepped into this brand-new template, I would be activating these codes within the entire Divine Feminine consciousness, as we are all one. And I also knew that all the sisters and brothers who were working with me on a personal level would be the first to receive these upgraded codes.

Even though I felt angry with my beloved for treating me in this dismissive way, I also felt an exceptional amount of gratitude, as I understood that there would be no way that I would come to this revelation without having had that experience. And not only was this experience benefiting me, but it was also going to benefit an entire collective of Divine Feminines.

I was truly grateful. This could be perceived as an affliction of the awakened. We always understand the higher reasons why everything happens to us, good and bad. And we always understand that we are never, ever a victim and that if we experience anything adverse, there are very, very important lessons in it for us, which will not only affect us but will affect the entire collective and all future generations.

Walking down the road in the rain working with the Red Circle technique, my life changed completely, since I knew that I would never, ever chase after a man again. I would truly make God happy by slipping into the vibration of magnetism, remembering fully that I am the awakened Divine Feminine and it is definitely not my role to go out hunting and searching for the masculine.

It is absolutely my role to focus on becoming the most exquisite and extraordinary version of myself through facing, loving and deeply integrating my shadow self, through aligning with source energy, through awakening spiritually, through becoming the observer of my monkey mind, through committing to a spiritual practice, and through saying no to any crumbs thrown my way.

I have brought through an extremely powerful and life-changing meditation programme that teaches you how to work deeply with the Red Circle technique.

Please see the accompanying workbook which includes meditations and exercises that will hugely support your transformation. For more information and how to order, please see the resources pages at the back of this book.

CHAPTER 3

Devotion as the New Relationship Template

As soon as I began working with the Red Circle technique, it became apparent to me that I was entirely responsible for the situation that I was in with my beloved.

Unbeknownst to me, my true love/my divine beloved already existed, and was fully available to serve me, but his sacred energy could only be accessed on a particular frequency band. Let's call that a 5th-dimensional frequency band.

Prior to my awakening, it became extremely apparent that I was not aligned or indeed on the same vibrational frequency as my divine beloved, as I was perfectly willing and calibrated towards accepting crumbs. Yet God had created it that my beloved was designed to saturate me in devotion.

In my revelation, I discovered that if I was willing to accept the bare minimum from the divine masculine, then I would never be a vibrational match to my sacred union, which already existed on a higher dimensional level, it was simply my duty and my responsibility to become a vibrational match to it.

It was obvious to me that I had to uplevel my personal vibration in all ways, particularly around my expectations of what I would and would not allow into my sacred space when it came to divine relationships.

When I had that experience with the man I was in love with, I realised that it was indeed where my vibration was attuned to, which was the reason why I wasn't aligning with my divine partner.

I was shown that I had a huge amount of work to do in terms of up-levelling my relationship with my own self-worth.

As soon as I discovered this, I worked diligently with the Red Circle technique, drawing circle upon circle around myself, and staking my claim that only a man that comes forward with the energy of recognition and devotion is allowed into my sacred space.

I used the power of affirmations and spellcasting to deeply embed this truth into my subconscious mind and psychic field.

Through repetition and deep intention work, I was able to massively transform my relationship with accepting crumbs very quickly, as I realised that it was 100% my responsibility why I wasn't attracting the relationship that my heart desired.

Of course, as with everything in life, I was not a victim of circumstance. The Universe was simply mirroring to me my own vibration and my own expectations.

So, armed with all these insights, I completely and absolutely let it go. I transcended the part of me that was accustomed to receiving crumbs, and I found myself in a new vibrational timeline, whereby only devotion and recognition of the divine goddess that I am would suffice.

This was a huge revelation for me and had a massive knock-on effect with my community, as I was able to coach many, many women to hugely transform and uplevel their own relationship with their self-worth regarding their personal relationships.

I realised that my divine beloved is alive and well, and is eternally transmitting his frequency in Devotion FM. It became obvious to me that the only way I was going to be able to come into sacred union with him was when I fully remembered that I was worthy to receive devotion, and thus only allow devotional energy into my sacred energetic space.

I hope that you are receiving insights and codes from reading these sacred words, and I pray for you to remember that you are never, ever a victim. The Universe is always responding to your vibrational input and output, and your life is a reflection of your beliefs and vibrations.

Therefore, you can easily read what is going on in your subconscious mind by simply looking at your life and ascertaining how fulfilled you are in each area of your life.

If you are unfulfilled in the area of romantic relationships, then it would be a very, very good moment to take an inventory of your beliefs around your expectations around romantic relationships.

CHAPTER 4

Recognising Our Needs as the Divine Feminine

Many of us have come from families whereby the divine feminine has taken on the role of Martyre. Many of us have witnessed our mothers and grandmothers sacrificing their individual needs, generation after generation, for everyone else in the family.

This is a very deep and powerful programming that has been taken on board by many divine feminines and has resulted in many of us barely even being able to register what our needs are.

Very often our unconscious needs are to keep everyone happy, to keep everyone well. And because of this natural default setting, we very often do not acknowledge what our own needs are. Additionally, if we were to take out a sheet of paper with all our beloved family members and start writing our needs, for most of us women, our needs would not even make it onto the sheet of paper.

This is an affliction that has been passed on for generations ad infinitum and is experienced by many women all over the world in many, many cultures. This does not serve us and is definitely not serving our children and our grandchildren.

We need to rise now as the divine feminines that we are, as the goddesses that we are, and take full ownership and responsibility of our value and worth, recognising that we are innocent daughters of God, and Mother-Father God has bestowed upon us all the gifts of the Kingdom and Queendom of Heaven.

We must understand that currently, we live in a world that will not willingly recognise this in us. Therefore, we have to step up and claim this remembrance on an individual level.

Please see this chapter in the book as an invitation for you to entirely release your belief system, which has enabled you to accept crumbs in your relationships. And please understand that you are powerful and you are magnetic and that you can easily attract a relationship that is templated with the codes of devotion and true love.

You are worthy of that.

You are God's daughter. You are God's son. You are truly worthy to receive all the deepest and most profound riches of the Kingdom and Queendom of Heaven.

May you absorb these words. May you allow these words to imprint your frontal cortex, enabling the frequencies of this message to effortlessly make their way into your heart consciousness, to empower the knowing and the voice of your heart, which stands proudly and unequivocally in remembrance of your perpetual divinity and worth as a divine daughter and son of our eternal Creator.

I pray that you absorb these keys and these codes as your own, and you absorb them for your children and your grandchildren. Please know you have my deepest blessings with you on this journey of remembrance.

Onwards to the next chapter.

CHAPTER 5

Magnetism

When we are sharing about the Rose and exploring deeply the codes of remembrance regarding our true value and worth and having conversations about the powerful ways that we can sweeten our nectar, a core aspect of what we are speaking about is intricately connected to spiritual magnetism.

Let us now go into an exploration of what this is, according to what I've been shown by my spiritual ascension team.

It is important to remember that in all areas we can approach our relationships to this reality utilising our masculine energy, our feminine energy, or both.

When we meet someone who is very stuck and orientated in their masculine energy, they often burn out very quickly, as they habitually place all their attention on seeking external sources of confirmation regarding the validating of one's self. This makes it such that their attention is often overly focused and orientated towards action and doing, which can lead to imbalance and burnout.

Someone who is deeply orientated in their masculine energy spends a lot of energy hustling for clients, hustling for partners, and hustling for deals.

When I use the word hustling, I am referring to a core belief that drives lack consciousness. A core belief that you do not have the magnetic power to attract the perfect person, perfect job opportunity or perfect business partner into your reality. And so, therefore, you must utilise all your energy on taking externally based actions in order to manifest your dream partner or business deal.

This is what I refer to as hustling. However, when we are in that mode, we step out of the vibration of magnetism, as we are unconsciously buying into the idea that we need to do something external in order to manifest the fulfilment of our dreams. Thus demonstrating to the Universe that we do not believe that we already possess that which we wish to experience, which as we all know is the master key to manifestation.

Of course, it is always appropriate for us to work on a masculine level, within reason and balance, in order to manifest our heart's desires.

It is always astute to remember that you can never manifest anything sitting on your backside doing nothing. There has to be an element of action. However, the problem arises when one is only orientated in one's masculine energy.

Someone who is hugely orientated in their masculine energy will be sending out direct messages into inboxes, putting a huge amount of energy on social media, and will spend a vast amount of time searching for a partner on apps or in other ways.

As you can see from these examples, there is a large focus on obsessively taking actions in order to manifest your heart's desires.

If you are a person that often acts in this way, this is an invitation for you to understand that very often this is coming from a vibration of lack. You have temporarily forgotten that we live in a great and benevolent Universe, and that in order to manifest anything in our reality, it is appropriate that we work with our masculine energy, which puts out to the Universe, that which we wish to manifest, then we must work with our feminine energy, which gives us permission to drop very deeply into our magnetic core, in order to attract everything our heart desires.

On my path of spiritual awakening, I quickly understood that I had a lot of work to do in terms of harnessing my feminine energy. Being a product of a patriarchal society, I had picked up many beliefs and indoctrinations that had programmed me to be extremely action-orientated towards searching and seeking externally for that which I wished to manifest.

When I had that experience with the man who I was in love with, which I shared with you all at the beginning of this book, I realised that I was completely neglecting my feminine essence and magic. I had completely forgotten the memo that we live in a benevolent and abundant Universe, and that everything that I wish to manifest already exists on a higher dimensional realm of consciousness. All I need to do is align with the knowing and the feeling of what it feels like to experience that which I wish to manifest, in order to draw it into my reality.

I realised that the role of the divine feminine is to be the Rose. The Rose doesn't have to do anything to be loved. The Rose simply exists. The Rose simply is. And through her beingness, she is worthy of love. She is worthy of nurturing. She is worthy of being nourished.

I realised that part of the patriarchal programming agenda had enforced an idea upon me that I wasn't the Rose and that I had to work and hustle in order to attract that which I wished to experience in my reality. In effect, I was programmed to be the bee: to go out hunting and searching for that which I wished to experience.

My spirit team teaches me through downloads and visions. And the day I experienced this profound download, my higher self team showed me very explicitly the truth: that my divine feminine essence is a Rose, and in and of herself is exquisitely beautiful and worthy of love.

I realised that within the Rose there is a nectar, and it is my job to ensure the nectar is as sweet as it possibly can be. I will devote the next chapter of this book to speaking about ways that I have discovered to sweeten our nectar.

I realised this was all an internal phenomenon. It was an internal plateau that I had to reach within my own being. This revelation absolutely completely changed my life. And I very quickly learned my true value and my true self-worth as an awakened divine feminine.

I eradicated and entirely collapsed all timelines whereby I was programmed to run after and hunt a man. And I realised that this had been a grave mistake that I was making energetically on my path to fulfilling relationships.

When you realise who you truly are, you will realise absolutely everything. You will realise that who we are is very simple and pure. And this matrix has sought to complicate and deeply confuse everyone's true and perpetual identity as children of eternal love.

When I had that awakening and revelation, I fully and completely remembered that I am worthy of love, simply by the fact that I exist; simply in the fact that God created me, deemed me worthy of love.

I allowed myself to drop into my magnetic energy. Embodying the truth of this was so freeing and so relaxing and it felt so right.

It felt like I was realigning myself with the true song of creation, through remembering my true value and worth.

CHAPTER 6

Sweeten our Nectar

On this journey of awakening and reclaiming our full remembrance of the truth, that the divine feminine is worthy of devotion, recognition and indeed everything her heart desires, we are brought to the subject matter of the nectar that resides within the core of the divine feminine's being.

This powerful and important nectar contains codes that the divine feminine promised she would activate within her own etheric field so that her true divine counterpart would find her in this matrix.

In order to fully align herself with the deepest and sweetest nectar of her being, she promised her beloved that she would remember her eternal sovereignty. She promised him that she would place her crown on her head and stand tall as an awakened daughter of God in full Remembrance; that sustenance, life force and alignment is sourced from within her own heart consciousness.

She would stand tall as a leader, remembering her duty to prioritise constant nurturing and nourishing of the sweet nectar that is her vibrational signature, which is intrinsically connected to her beloved on a subconscious level.

What does it mean when we say sweeten our nectar?

On that fateful day, when I walked away from the man I loved, I absolutely, completely remembered at the deepest cellular level that I am a Rose.

I remembered implicitly that it is my job to rest in the joy of my exquisite beauty and knowledge of who I truly am.

I understood that as I dropped into this frequency of Remembrance, that this would subconsciously send codes and signals to my divine masculine to inform him that I truly am ready for our divine sacred union.

I experienced revelation after revelation, and my team showed me the preparatory work that I could do to sweeten the nectar of the Rose that I am.

I understood that this means truly and absolutely loving myself while restoring any fragmented shadow aspects back home to my heart consciousness.

I understood that sweetening my nectar meant transcending the need for anyone's approval, and perpetually remaining absolutely free and committed to being the most beautiful and exquisite version of myself. Knowing that God sees me in every second and every moment of my existence.

Sweetening our nectar also refers to fully and completely remembering that we are intimately connected to our beloved on a subconscious level and that as we transform and uplevel our spiritual vibration and capacity for gnosis, this has an immediate knock-on effect with our divine beloved, who then begins to experience his own transformation in order to uplevel with us.

This is very much connected to the research that has been carried out with an atom that has been split into two.

Scientists discovered that if one of the atoms changes its direction, regardless of how far the other atom has travelled away from it, the other atom will also change direction at exactly the same time.

This shows us how intricately connected we all are on an atomic level, and whenever we go through a powerful transformational upgrade, this is always experienced by our divine counterparts.

Please see my book *Twin Flames & The Event* where I go into extraordinary detail explaining about twin flames and the importance of the Divine Couple in terms of the ascension of one's consciousness.

When we sweeten our nectar, it means that we are no longer ruled and swept along by our monkey mind. We understand that the ego is not the amigo, and many of the thoughts that run through our consciousness are very often connected to the collective, and often have nothing to do with us, and are therefore impersonal to us.

Someone who has extremely sweet nectar has fully remembered this and has mastered becoming the observer of their monkey mind.

Whenever we do this; whenever we detach ourselves from the egoic narrative, like a beautiful golden bird, we realise that we are eternally free and have always been free. We implicitly understand that the ego was simply an illusion. It was an illusionary cage that was fooling us into believing that we were trapped.

When we have mastered becoming the observer of our ego identity, we deeply come home to the place of perpetual and abiding grace. There is nothing sweeter for our nectar than this grace that is being spoken about here, as this is the grace of liberation, of freedom, of happiness; of eternal connection with source energy.

At this point, I would like to remind all the divine feminines reading this book, that my spiritual team have repeatedly shown me that for the most part, the divine masculines did not want to return back to the earthly plane, as the conditioning for the divine masculine has been even more challenging than it has been for the divine feminine.

But we, as the divine feminine, promised the divine masculine that we would awaken, that we would sweeten our nectar, in order to come to a vibratory place of magnetism and attraction, whereby our divine beloved will very easily be able to find us and locate us within the matrix.

It is very important that everyone reading these words takes a moment to remember this promise that you made to your divine counterpart, that you would fully remember that you are a goddess, you are a god, and you are an innocent child of the divine, and you are here to shine as brightly as you possibly can.

Someone who has intensely sweet nectar does not seek permission to shine like an illuminated million-watt bulb. We shine because we wish to share our energy with our brothers and sisters, understanding that this has been a very dark realm for human souls. And so by shining, we are bringing sunshine and light to all our brothers and sisters, which is a profound act of generosity and service.

One who has sweet nectar is fully aligned and at home with this truth and remembrance and does not wait for permission to shine like a beacon of light. And is thus easily located by one's divine beloved.

CHAPTER 7

———

Let Go of The Story

In my experience, one of the ways to ensure eternal and perpetual happiness is to entirely let go of our story.

What is our story?

Our story is our third-dimensional identity, which we have created on a soul level with Mother-Father God, in order to have a personality and an experience within the third dimension.

Very often our story is constructed from the wounds that we experienced in early childhood. Be they abuse, trauma, abandonment, or betrayal, our early experiences act like a filter obscuring our perception of reality and giving us a false idea of who we truly are.

The third dimension has sought to keep us all identified with our stories; this wounded aspect of ourselves, and it is this which very often keeps everyone on a perpetual cycle of suffering.

In one of my mini-enlightenment experiences in 2011, after watching a powerful documentary of many amazing motivational speakers sharing their wisdom, I realised clearly that I was addicted to continuously regurgitating my story at every opportunity that presented itself.

I was addicted to being a victim, and I was addicted to proving to God that I was a victim. My default setting was: "Please feel sorry for me God, and give me what I need because I'm a victim and you need to help me".

I realised that I was shamelessly addicted to my story. And I realised that as a magical being, the more I was sharing my story with everyone, and perpetuating my identification with it, the more suffering I created in my life.

So, after watching this incredible documentary of motivational speakers, I decided that I would put my story down once and for all.

I decided that I would never, ever bring it up and talk about it ever again. That I would do some sort of ceremony to release it and let it go. I would like to say thank you to my story for getting me to this point of realising that it is basically my ego narrative – a false identity construct that I have created in order to be in a constant and perpetual state of fear and separation from Source energy.

Letting go of being attached to one's story is an extremely confronting moment, but I cannot recommend it highly enough.

I would say that I am a top athlete when it comes to spiritual instruction and application. As soon as I realise what I have to do, I will do it.

At that moment, I absolutely, unequivocally decided I would never, ever pick up my story again and use it to moan to God about how terrible my life is. I realised the extent of my addiction to doing this in all of my relationships, and how most of my relationships were built upon this unspoken agreement that that is what we speak about: our woes and disappointments with the Universe and God at large.

So at that moment in 2011, I put down my story and I have never, ever picked it up to this day. People in my community wouldn't even know what my story is. No one even knows what my story is. Sometimes I have to dig deep myself, to even remember what my story is.

My incarnational wounding, otherwise known as my story, was triggered recently by the very shocking passing of a beloved of mine. This experience triggered the old wounding associated with my story, which, now we're on the subject, is connected to the physical abandonment of the masculine.

My story was triggered by never meeting my father. This attracted experiences of great and deep abandonment with many men that I loved.

I'm writing this book in the aftermath of the shocking passing of a beloved of mine whom I have just recently come out of a relationship with. He's always with me, and I feel like he's Angelically with me and my heart at all times.

I feel his warmth and love encased in these words and pouring through these words onto the page. He's bringing his wisdom and knowledge and vibration from the higher dimensional realms now, as I transmit this reminder to all of us.

There is no separation.

Please consider this chapter as an invitation for you to put down your story.

There is a meditation that goes along with this chapter that will assist you to put down your story. Please see the link at the back of the book if you wish to gift yourself this powerful upgrade experience.

Once you put down your story and commit to never picking it up again, you will realise that you were expending an extraordinary amount of important spiritual energy on being absorbed in thought forms that were not serving you or your highest good.

Once this addiction has ceased, and you finally start letting go of this desperate desire to moan all the time, you will quickly come into alignment with the benevolent force of creation: that which keeps the stars in their place and transforms a sperm and egg into a baby.

This is all part of how we become empty.

When we let go of our story, this is when we become empty.

We become free to simply, fully enjoy all the glorious gifts the present moment holds for us.

I would say that now is an appropriate moment to ask the question.... What does emptiness mean? What does being empty actually mean?

Emptiness means becoming non-identified and free of your story.

Every single one of us has a story. You have a story, I have a story, we all have a sob story, but your eternal glory and true identity as God's most beloved child will never be accessed through identification with that which is known as your story.

To be empty means that you are simply present as a child: present and grateful for the opportunities that are presented to you in every single moment.

When we are fully present in our body, cherishing every moment of having this experience of being in a body and experiencing life on Earth, we are truly cherishing the gift of the present moment.

It is very important at this juncture that we all remember that Mother-Father God has created it so that all instruments are empty, and there is a reason for that.

It is my understanding that an instrument such as a guitar or a flute or a drum must be empty so that it can be filled with the light of divine grace.

Therefore, please understand that coming home to the Remembrance of the divine self means absolutely and truly letting go of your story and becoming empty like an instrument.

Please understand that you are an incredibly delightful, enlightened, exquisite, sacred, and eternal being. Mother-Father God sees you in your nakedness and beauty, in your childlike innocence, and it is your duty to recognise this in all your brothers and sisters.

When we understand our innocence, we understand the Trinity. We understand that we have a parental aspect and a divine child self, and it is our duty to look after our divine child self through having clear and sacred boundaries, ensuring that she is always safe, she is always protected and that her safety and her well-being is the number one priority in our life.

When you put down your story, you very, very quickly align with the highest frequencies of creation. And may you be reminded that it is very important that you adopt a spiritual practise in order to keep your vibration very high and pristine.

CHAPTER 8

Boundaries and the Trinity

In one's journey of Awakening to the truth of our true value and worth, we will have to face the fact that many times in our lives, and in previous lives, we allowed actions and behaviours towards us that did not serve us or our family's greatest good.

This has all been part of the programming and indoctrination of the third dimension, which has sought to entirely eradicate the voice of the Divine Feminine. However, the Goddess has now risen and she speaks in these pages, and so, therefore, I would like to devote the next chapter of this book to highlighting the importance of boundaries.

A huge part of the programming of the third dimension has eradicated the important and intuitive voice of the Divine Feminine. She, who is in deep union with her heart consciousness.

Her voice has been belittled and silenced.

As part of this programming, the Divine Feminine has been trained to believe that on some levels she is blessed to even be able to speak, never mind setting clear boundaries for her own protection and expansion.

It is only when one truly awakens out of the matrix to the perpetual Remembrance of one's innocence as a child of God, that one is able to come home to the truth of the Trinity, and the automatic innerstanding of boundaries that comes along with this.

The Trinity represents the Holy Mother, the Holy Father, and the Christ/Sophia child.

In one's Kundalini awakening, many things are internally realised, one of the most important being the deep understanding of the Trinity and the knowledge that: "I am the Trinity". Please see my book *Twin Flames & The Event* where I devote many chapters to speaking in great depth on the intricacies of the Kundalini Awakening and experience.

With this knowledge comes the deep understanding that I have a fully alive and embodied parental aspect whose sole job and responsibility is to parent the Christ/Sophia child aspect of my being.

As soon as I awakened to that, I quickly understood the necessity of having boundaries. As it was quite clear to me that it was my duty to protect and look after my eternal divine child-self. She who is deeply, absolutely and completely adored and revered by God our eternal creator.

That was my full and complete Remembrance.

When you remember that you have an internal and eternal child aspect that is deeply beloved by Mother-Father God, you understand that Mother-Father God has given you the duty to parent this child self. One of the ways that we do that is by becoming guardian of what we allow vibrationally into our psychic field.

This powerful sacred Remembrance automatically activates sacred boundaries: boundaries around the energy that you will allow into your sacred space.

This is related to the types of relationships that you will allow into your sacred space, the types of music, the types of conversations, the types of food, the types of media. It is all intricately connected to boundaries and what you will and will not allow vibrationally into your sacred space.

A huge part of the programming of the third dimension has been to belittle our intuitive voice and dismiss the knowing within us that commands and demands respect and honour at all times.

One awakens to the necessity and importance of boundaries when one fully realises that one has a parental aspect whose soul duty is to care for their divine child aspect. It is the parental aspect's job to keep the child aspect safe, keep her happy, and ensure that she has lots and lots of fun.

When you understand this, your relationship with boundaries is automatic, because you realise that you are here to protect your inner child, and you will do everything in your power to fully and absolutely fulfil that sacred agreement.

CHAPTER 9

Guardian of your Spiritual Vibration

I would like to now devote this chapter to speaking about the importance and necessity of becoming the guardian of your spiritual vibration. There's so much to speak about on this subject matter that it is tricky to know where to start.

Being the guardian of your spiritual vibration refers to being the guardian of all of the inputs and outputs you allow into your physical, emotional, mental, and spiritual reality.

This refers to:

The music that you allow into your space, the media you allow into your space, the relationships you allow into your space, the foods you allow into your space, and the environments you allow yourself to dwell in.

If you are allowing toxic programming to infiltrate your sacred consciousness, you are not being the guardian of your spiritual vibration. It is very important to understand, if you're reading these words, that enlightenment, although extremely simple, is only attained by the true Olympic spiritual athletes, who diligently commit to the teachings and tools that are shared in this book and in other sacred scriptures.

Those who commit diligently to harnessing and purifying their perception in order to receive the messages from their intuition, unfiltered and untainted by the ego's false perception.

It is very important for you to understand the fundamental necessity of being the guardian of your inner child self. It is your duty to protect her on all levels regarding the art that she looks at, the music that she listens to, and the media that she consumes.

In some ways, it could even be argued that if we allow ourselves to consume mainstream media, this is actually abusive to our souls and abusive to our inner child self.

A perfect illustration of when we are not being guardians of our spiritual vibration is when we allow propaganda and the evil narrative of the mainstream media into our divine heart and consciousness.

There are many ways that we can actively engage in raising our spiritual vibration. One way is to throw away your TV and limit yourself to zero mainstream media, and instead look for high vibrational news sources and outlets of information.

Here are some of my top tips to raise your vibration:

Spend a great deal of time in nature. Allow yourself to be reset by nature, away from your phone, away from your computer.

Allow the vibrations of nature to reset you.

Walk barefoot on the earth as much as possible. Feel that beautiful, sacred connection with Mother Earth, knowing that she wants to feel you and you want to feel her. You both want to feel each other. Give her that gift of your beautiful, sacred feet on the earth.

Drink very high vibrational water and eat only organic food. Practice exercise, deep breathing, yoga and meditation, regularly.

Surround yourself with high vibrational music, particularly 432 hertz, sacred mantras and bhajans, holy music, godly music, happy celebratory and ecstatic music.

Realise that all life is Art and that the world deserves you to show up in your greatest beauty, glamour and gorgeousness in every moment.

Make an effort to shine as brightly as you possibly can, knowing that you wear your crown with pride for all your brothers and sisters who have forgotten their holy divinity and are under the hypnotic spell of the third-dimensional dualistic illusion.

Every morning when you wake up, choose to be in service to your brothers and sisters. Choose to be in a positive energetic frequency, practice uplifting your tone and passing that energetic frequency on in the supermarket, in the garage and all the shops that you enter.

Sing, dance, play music, move your body, be in community, spend time with friends, laugh, watch happy funny movies and comedians.

Watch and consume media that raises your vibration and brings you happiness, joy and laughter.

Take care of your body with beautiful healing plants and minerals. Cleanse your body, keep it alkaline, and eat lots of fruit and vegetables. Take necessary supplements whenever you feel deficient in any area.

Bathe in spring water. Remember that spring water is one of the closest elements we have to living light. And when we grant ourselves the gift of bathing in spring water, we are giving ourselves a very, very deep spiritual and etheric cleanse. This is the top way to raise our spiritual vibration.

Work with the law of attraction: Create crystal grids, create intentions.

Live your life as though all of your dreams have manifested and have already come true.

Be in excitement mode, be in preparation mode.

Share this book with as many people as you can. Spread this beautiful, positive message and vibration to awaken as many brothers and sisters as we possibly can.

There are so many ways. I could go on for days.

There can be no slip-ups on the path to enlightenment: it's all or nothing. You're all in or you're all out.

So if you're not ready to go all-in, I would say don't even bother. But when you are ready to truly go all in, put down your story, absolutely, and choose to completely let it go by being masterful and vigilant around protecting and nurturing your highest vibration.

God bless you for all your sacred work and for aligning in this beautiful moment whereby you are receiving these words.

CHAPTER 10

My Awakening

I really could not go a chapter further without stressing the importance of reading my first book, *Twin Flames & The Event*. This is the foundation book for all my work and all my teachings. So if you are reading this far and you haven't yet read that book, I would urge you to please go ahead and gift yourself it now. So many of the teachings, concepts and truths that I will speak about repeatedly in this book are explained in great detail in *Twin Flames & The Event*.

When I was 21 years of age, I experienced an extremely powerful and life-changing Kundalini awakening on top of a Himalayan mountain very close to Mount Kailash in India, while chanting repetitively the mantra *Om Namah Shivaya*.

At that moment on the mountain, my third eye blasted open and I realised that I was in the presence of God, as well as many ascended beings who were in ecstatic celebration that another soul had awoken out of the matrix.

I felt the presence of John Lennon, Bob Marley, Gandhi, Mother Mary, Mary Magdalene, Archangel Michael, Babaji, and many, many saints and ascended beings. They were all there in that moment in ecstatic celebration with me when my third eye blasted open, and I truly remembered who I am.

I remembered that everything is one. That every blade of grass, every grain of sand is intricately woven into the perfection of creation. I remembered that each and every one of us is an extraordinarily, important and beautiful masterpiece. We are direct fractals of God; the oneness of creation.

My ego died and I was reborn into the presence and recognition of the eternal Mother and Father of all Creation: that which created us, as well as all the stars in the sky, all the trees, and indeed absolutely everything.

At that moment, I was with my spiritual brother, Christopher. And I looked into his eyes and I recognised the Christ self that dwelled eternally in him. I fully recognised him as God's innocent son, and in that moment of recognition, I experienced the full ascension of my consciousness and I experienced the twin flame merge with him, at the age of 21, on top of a Himalayan mountain.

When I saw the Christed self in him, I knew deeply and emphatically that this was a reflection of the feminine Christed self that dwelled within me.

The moment I realised that, I also realised that the Christed self dwelled equally in every single one of God's creations, as Mother-Father God is a great and perfect God and has no favourites. We are all equal, direct offspring of God. And we are all equally loved, precious, sacred, exquisite and powerful.

My heart opened like a million-petalled lotus flower, to the full and absolute celebration of ecstatic God-consciousness. And I resided in that state for six months, during my stay in India. Upon returning to the UK, I experienced what I often refer to as a very, very gentle landing back into the western world, holding a fully awakened state of consciousness.

Since 1995, I've been navigating holding this higher consciousness within this particular matrix structure.

On top of the mountain, encyclopedias of knowledge were downloaded into my consciousness. Without a doubt, the most powerful Remembrance for me was regarding the innocence of all Mother-Father God's creations.

It was glaringly obvious to me that the programming of the third-dimensional matrix had sought to create a false belief that we, as God's most beloved and innocent creations, are sinners and inherently scarred.

Indeed, it was apparent to me that this programming caused great suffering in God's heart, to know that this false, dark agenda was being inflicted and imprinted upon His and Her most sacred, beloved children of the earth.

I awakened to so much truth about the nature of reality; the nature of God-consciousness, Christ-consciousness, what is eternity, what is love.

Prior to my awakening, these were all two-dimensional concepts that I really had no direct experience of. I had no direct experience of timelessness. I had had no direct experience of oneness, no direct experience of Eternity or forever. Yet in my awakening, the veil parted and I understood deeply, essentially, eternally and implicitly what all these sacred states of consciousness truly are.

This was an extraordinary experience that entirely transformed my reality.

I had awakened to the perpetual Remembrance of the innocence of all Mother-Father God's children. And I had fully and completely remembered that we were born in love, we will die in love, and it is our duty in every moment, to be present to the glory of God's love.

When I speak of the Self, I speak of the pure, untainted Self. The Self prior to the agreements that we all made to incarnate into the third dimension. I am referring to your eternal and innocent Self, the aspect of your being that God holds very, very deeply in Her heart.

So, therefore, the foundation of this book is such that it comes forward with a recognition that you are a divine, innocent child of God and Goddess. And it is through this sacred Remembrance and Atonement to the truth of who you are, that all the codes of self-worth are fully restored back to you.

The eternal You who is perpetually unencumbered by the egoic consciousness, which has sought to create a false filter over the truth of who you are.

It is your role to put down all of the false ideas and distortions that were placed upon your sacred consciousness, which you as a divine child willingly absorbed, being the good girl or boy that you truly are at your core.

May we all now fully remember that our good nature was used against us. But from this moment onwards, we can choose to release all contracts pertaining to the allowing of our sacred consciousness to ever be hijacked again.

It would serve everyone reading these words to do a powerful ceremony where you fully release the archonic hijacking of your personal consciousness stream.

Please know that I have created a meditation that accompanies this chapter that will assist you to fully release all lower-dimensional hijacking of your consciousness.

Please see the accompanying workbook which includes meditations and exercises that will hugely support your transformation. For more information and how to order, please see the resources pages at the back of this book.

When we truly release ourselves from the third-dimensional hijacked matrix and align ourselves with the vibration of God, we quickly align with the vibration of creation. The same vibration that keeps the birds singing and the leaves growing on the trees every year. It is what turns an egg and sperm into a baby.

There is a particular hum of creation that is high and benevolent. And it is vital that we come to the zero-point field, in order to have our perception absolutely, completely purified and restored.

For it is only when our perception is purified, that we see our brothers and sisters in the true light of who they truly are, as innocent children of God.

It is through the reflection of our brothers and sisters that we recognise our own eternal innocence.

To start you on your path of recognising the Christed self that dwells in all, I highly recommend focusing your attention on babies. They unapologetically shine the eternal beam of the Christed Self. They will remind you of your true nature .

This is the aspect of the self that God sees in all of us: the baby self, the primary self, the child self. God sees every single one of us and all his and her creations as the glorious, innocent children that we truly are.

So, therefore, please understand that this is the foundational teaching of this entire book: the understanding and recognition of the perpetual innocence of each of us as children of God.

CHAPTER 11

The Zero-Point Field

Another key component and foundational aspect of the teaching of this book is based upon the understanding of the zero-point field of consciousness.

What exactly is the zero-point field of consciousness?

As divine beings, we reside on a consciousness level eternally on the higher dimensional realms.

This higher dimensional realm of consciousness is also known as unity consciousness and is also known as fifth-dimensional consciousness and above.

Each of us who have returned back to the earthly plane made a soul contract while sitting at the feet of Mother-Father God to reincarnate into a lower-dimensional realm. In this case, this particular realm being the third-dimensional Earth realm.

At the moment of incarnation into the third-dimensional realm, we choose to take on the experience of dropping our vibrational frequency in order to blend in and be calibrated into the third-dimensional reality.

Part of the contract of arriving in the third dimension is that we experience amnesia of sorts that blocks our sacred Remembrance of our true multi-dimensionality.

Therefore, the zero-point field is the actual 'truth of who you are'.

Beyond duality, beyond this dimensional realm.

In your eternal State of Consciousness, you are eternally at one with the zero-point field.

The third-dimensional programming perpetuates the notion of life and death, of you and me, of separation and ownership. So much of our language is addicted to perpetuating the notion of duality and separation.

This is what is referred to as lower-dimensional consciousness.

As you embark on your Ascension journey, working with DNA trigger numbers such as 11.11, 144, 5.5 etc, astrology, and all the amazing tools and codes that are out there to assist you on your spiritual ascension path, you will be triggered to awaken out of the dualistic mindset of the third dimension. Your consciousness will start questioning the constraints and dominant beliefs of the third dimension, and you will notice that you are beginning to rise in consciousness from the third dimension to the fourth dimension.

This is why I am so strongly guided by spirit to host my Global Transmissions on numerological portal dates such as the Lions Gate which takes place on the 8th August - the 8:8 portal. These monthly online ceremonies are attended by up to 800 people each month. For more information and to book, please see the resources pages at the back of this book.

The fourth dimension is still riddled with duality but it is a much more powerful and magical realm of consciousness than the third dimension.

When your consciousness reaches the fourth dimension this is definitely a progression and marks a powerful expansion within your vibrational set point, with the result that you are one step closer to fifth-dimensional consciousness, which is also known as unity consciousness.

At some point within your evolutionary expansion, you will come home to the memory that you are everything that you have ever sought. *And that will be the moment of your enlightenment.*

You will realise that you are a multidimensional Avatar angelic soul, who has been programmed to believe and identify with the false notion that you are a superficial third-dimensional being, when nothing could be further from the truth. Your consciousness is eternal and beyond the egoic narrative; beyond the identification with the story.

You remember unequivocally that your soul is eternally plugged into the zero-point field and at one with God and all that is.

The journey of Ascension is extraordinarily multi-layered, deep and complex, where we awaken out of the false notion and illusion of duality consciousness, also known as third-dimensional consciousness, into the truth of oneness, unity consciousness, and sacred union.

The zero-point field is the present moment. Being empty is being present in the present moment, and of course, we all know there's a reason why Mother-Father God called it the 'present'. Because every child appreciates the present moment and is at one with all the sensual possibilities of every single moment.

CHAPTER 12

Kundalini

One's perpetual and abiding spiritual awakening is intricately connected to the Kundalini energy, the Kundalini merge, and the Hieros Gamos. (Please see my book *Twin Flames & The Event* for a full and deep explanation into the Kundalini energy and the sacred merge that takes place at the base of the spine for those of us that sign up for the spiritual Ascension path).

I will briefly explain here:

Your Kundalini energy resides at the base of your spine.

When we incarnate we make a deep subconscious agreement in our pre-birth state, that our Kundalini energy will remain dormant at the base of our spine, until the moment of our Spiritual Awakening.

At some point on our spiritual Ascension path, the two dormant Kundalini serpents will be triggered to awaken and finally merge and come into Sacred union.

At that moment in the dance of the sacred union of our Kundalini energy, we move out of duality consciousness into oneness, into Sacred union. This is the zero-point field. This is the level of consciousness that is experienced when you transcend dualistic third-dimensional consciousness.

It is very important that everyone understands that the teachings of this book are deeply embedded with enlightenment codes, designed to trigger, activate and awaken your DNA out of its long-term hypnosis and deep sleep to the full Remembrance of your innocence and glory as a divine child of God.

When one arrives at the zero-point field of consciousness, this is the gateway into fifth-dimensional consciousness. Fifth-dimensional consciousness is the opening point for sixth-, seventh-, eighth-, ninth-, tenth-, eleventh-, twelfth-dimensional consciousness, and above.

I will speak more about the fifth dimension in later chapters in this book, but I would highlight at this point, the importance of understanding that in order for one to truly come home to God-consciousness, it is absolutely imperative that one commits to becoming absolutely and completely empty.

CHAPTER 13

Spoken Word

It's the second day of writing this book, and I had a very auspicious conversation today with one of my best friends, who I happened to read the opening chapters of this book to.

That powerful conversation brought up so many topics of importance, which I feel must share in this chapter.

We spoke for many, many hours, and as I look back on our conversation the most striking moment I remember is when we discussed her using the power of her voice to create the reality she wishes to experience in her romantic relationships.

We spoke about the importance of the Throat Chakra and the necessity to upgrade it in order to fully activate this centre.

It was such a fascinating conversation, as I had just started writing, and everything that we spoke about was specifically related to the subject matter of this book.

We spoke about purifying and cleansing her throat chakra, to get to the point whereby she is able to utilise the power of her voice to transform her vibrational reality from one where she is accepting crumbs to one whereby a full and absolute boundary is created around her, which states, from this moment on: "I no longer accept crumbs, I only accept devotion".

We spoke about how alchemical magic occurs when we utilise the power of the spoken word. This is the magical realm of spell casting.

We spoke about how the right use of language brings us into extremely magical realms of consciousness, enabling us to build and co-create our holographic version of reality, and thus experience it on the physical plane.

Each time we assert our boundaries, we rewrite every cellular imprint within our body that has accepted crumbs; that has accepted inconsistency, that has accepted non-commitment, that has accepted being last on the list.

When we use the power of our voice to speak into existence our sacred boundaries, we literally transform our vibrational experience of reality.

In our beautiful and in-depth conversation we spoke about this, and how for women this can often be so difficult, as so many of us have been entrained to wear the 'good girl hat'. The hat whereby we do not wish to attract disapproval from anyone in our reality, and therefore we will do everything not to rock the boat or attract potential disapproval.

However, this is one of the greatest afflictions known to humanity: the inability to stand in our truth and potentially court disapproval.

I am being guided at this moment to offer some context of the time period with which this book is being brought to you.

This book is being written at the time of the Great Awakening in the month of May in the year 2021.

Currently, we are in the process of witnessing many huge shifts taking place on the inner and outer planes.

It seems obvious to me that in these times, many of us are being tested to see whether we are able to use the power of our voice to step up and stand alone in our truth, regardless of other people's approval or disapproval.

During these powerful, monumental shifting times, it would seem that it is this specific issue that is sorting the wheat from the chaff.

It is glaringly obvious that currently there are so many in society that are going along with the fear-based narrative that is being perpetuated at every opportunity by the mainstream media. And at the same time there are so many that are truly awakening to their sovereignty and saying no to anything that goes against their intuition and higher self-knowing.

This is what is occurring for each of us, as we realise that in all our relationships we have the opportunity to wear the hat of seeking others' approval and thus neglecting our own truth, or we can put that hat down and burn it, so that we can stand tall in our absolute truth and sovereignty. We can then assert clearly our values and our expectations with regards to how we will be treated in our private and personal relationships.

May the words encoded in this chapter spark off codons within your own DNA patterning, enabling you to remember how powerful you are.

Every time you speak your truth you align with your heart, and you align with the happiness and the benevolent force of creation, which is what keeps the birdsong singing and keeps the stars in their places.

This is an invitation for you to truly allow yourself to step forward now, unafraid, able to speak clearly your boundaries, and remembering when you do that great magic occurs.

An alchemical transformation occurs at such a deep, profound cellular level that if only you could glimpse for one moment what lies in that vibrational reality, you would do it instantly.

You would say 'no' to anything that is not honouring and not recognising you as the embodiment of the Divine Feminine or the Divine Masculine.

May these words trigger the deep Remembrance of your holiness, of your divinity, of the sacred power of your word, and the necessity to give attention to your throat chakra, to upgrade your throat chakra and empower your throat chakra to speak its truth at this time of great planetary transformation.

We are each going through our own ascension process, transforming from a third-dimensional, approval-seeking caterpillar to a fifth-dimensional, absolutely 100% free sovereign butterfly.

The Earth, herself, is also going through this ascension process. Those souls that choose to stay in the fear vibration will not be ascending on this wave of this ascension cycle. They will be given another round of incarnations, in order to become ready to ascend in the next reincarnation cycle.

However, those souls that are truly ready to stand up and be counted regardless of the approval of anyone and everyone around them – these are the leaders of the new Earth.

The Earth is ascending, and we are all in the process of experiencing the ascension of Mother Earth.

We are all experiencing the ascension of our consciousness from 3D to 5D.

Mother Earth is experiencing the ascension of her consciousness from 3D to 5D.

Please read my book, *Twin Flames & The Event*, where I speak about this subject matter in great detail.

CHAPTER 14

Sovereignty

I would like to devote the next chapter of this book to speaking about the important foundational subject matter of sovereignty.

This book really could not have been written had I not understood deeply and implicitly what it means to be a truly sovereign being. And so I would like to now share with you some of my journey of how that occurred.

I highly recommend reading my book, *Twin Flames & The Event*, where I speak in great depth and great detail about the spiritual awakenings that have taken place in my lifetime.

Suffice to say, the spiritual awakenings that I have experienced have been so powerful and almighty that they have enabled me to fully and completely become consciously aware of the false programming of the dualistic third-dimensional matrix. As a result, I have been able to transcend the vibrational frequency of this said matrix.

When we incarnate into this dimensional realm, we all agree to take on the experience of having spiritual amnesia, which means we agree to forget our true eternal divine origins.

We all sign up with some sort of story, which keeps us entrapped and calibrated to the third-dimensional template of suffering. However, at some point within our evolutionary trajectory, if we are on the Awakening Ascension path we will experience a trigger. This could be a twin flame. This could be a beautiful song or poem. It could even be a view in nature that will trigger our Kundalini energy to come out of its dormant state, into its merged and unified state.

Once this sacred union occurs at the base of the spine, this is known as the Hieros Gamos, the inner alchemical merge.

Once this momentum occurs at the base of the spine, our consciousness transcends from being calibrated to the third-dimensional dualistic reality to the fifth-dimensional oneness template.

When our consciousness transcends and outgrows the third-dimensional dualistic timeline, we realise our true and perpetual nature as innocent children of God, that we were created at the moment of the Big Bang in the vibratory frequency of eternal love. And when our soul is complete with this mission, our body will return back to the earth and our soul will ascend back to God, to reside in perpetual love.

In our Ascension path, we realise that love is all that is. Love is synonymous with God and love is the true default setting of our soul consciousness.

We fully remember it is our duty and responsibility to be aligned with the frequency of love throughout our entire sojourn of this particular physical lifetime, and indeed all lifetimes forever and ever.

Therefore sovereignty refers to humanity, one-by-one detaching and disassociating themselves from the dualistic third-dimensional template and realising that they are an eternal, perpetual daughter or son of God the most high.

Once we realise our spiritual origins and we realise that indeed we are all carriers of the Holy Bloodline, it does not take long for us to be familiarised with the etheric crown that mother-father God has placed safely and patiently within our auric field, awaiting the moment of our awakening and empowerment that we may reach up into our etheric field and place our crown firmly on our own head.

At that moment when we place our crown on our head, we claim our sovereignty. We claim our Remembrance that we are innocent children of God.

In doing this we entirely release ourselves from the lower dimensional constructs and constraints of the third dimension. This refers to any governmental structures or any false rules, mandates or laws that are designed to keep us under the illusion of control within the third-dimensional matrix.

In that moment of awakening and sovereignty, we absolutely completely 100% transcend the need for any connection to the third-dimensional dualistic matrix system. Sovereignty is individuality. Sovereignty is your true birthright. Sovereignty is your true spiritual vibration. Sovereignty is the truth of who you are.

The opposite of sovereignty is slavery. And a huge part of the indoctrination of the third dimension has been to keep everyone entrapped in a comfortable agenda of slavery.

I read a quote recently and it said, "Birds trapped in a cage think birds that can fly are afflicted with an illness". This is a perfect example to illustrate what occurs for many people within the matrix who entirely forget the memo about sovereignty and the fact that we are all inherently powerful and extraordinary individualised sovereign beings.

If you have forgotten this notion, then you join the herd mentality and you give your power away to external forces, such as church leaders, governments, politicians, headteachers, doctors...

The true source of the knowledge within you exists within your own heart consciousness and your own intuition, and it is your duty to release all egotistical filters that have blocked your intuitive and heart-based knowing, so that you may become a clear vessel, able to receive the direct messages from your own inner Gnosis and intuition.

This is how a sovereign being moves through the world. We do not look for external authority figures with regards to our health, wellbeing, emotional state, or with regards to any rulership over our physical, mental, emotional, spiritual, physical or psychological being.

We understand that this is an extremely archaic construct and indeed a timeline that has now expired for us as a collective.

We are collectively now fully and completely stepping into our sovereignty and releasing all notions, codes and templates pertaining to our planetary connection to the slavery timeline.

So please understand there is no one coming to save you. You are your own saviour. There is no spiritual authority that has the power to give you permission to place your individual crown upon your head. That is your duty and your responsibility. So please take the words on this page as an invitation for you to wake up from the illusion of giving your power away and desperately needing to be a good girl or boy in order to not rock the boat or attract disapproval.

This attitude is not going to take you into fifth-dimensional unity consciousness. This attitude will keep you deeply entrenched in third-dimensional slavery consciousness.

I will speak more about the important subject matter of the programme of needing other people's approval in a later chapter in this book.

Please see the accompanying workbook where I have brought through a powerful meditation that will enable you to connect the Crown that has been positioned securely in your etheric field, awaiting a moment for you to reach into your etheric field to place it on your divine head. For more information and how to order, please see the resources pages at the back of this book.

CHAPTER 15

Surrender

I would like to devote this chapter to speaking about the subject of surrender. It took me a very long time to truly understand what surrender means, and I feel I have some real gems to share with you on this subject matter.

Surrender is synonymous with trust.

Surrender is the equivalent of a pregnant woman who knows at some point she will give birth. She doesn't know how, she doesn't know when, but she is in absolute trust that something which is absolutely unknown to her is 100% going to happen.

Therefore, the true essence of surrender in many ways is preparation. Preparing for that which we know is on its way.

For example, when we are in surrender we are in full trust, and if we are working with the law of attraction to manifest our divine counterpart then an extremely powerful action to take is to prepare our space to be ready for our beloved.

It is always auspicious to work with the energies of alignment, such as feng shui, sacred geomancy, or even buying furniture or homely goods for your beloved in the absolute trust and knowing that he or she is on their way.

This is surrender. This is trust. The Rose is in a perpetual state of surrender. The Rose knows that her only job is to be beautiful, to be still, be trusting, and be perfectly confident in her absolute divine exquisite presence.

The Rose remembers that she has it all, that God gave her more than enough to live in alignment and sustenance.

When we are in surrender, we are truly in the vibration of excitement and preparation. Excitement is an extremely high vibratory energetic space that is extremely magnetic. For all those working with the law of attraction, please know that this particular frequency band is highly recommended to activate, within one's energetic field.

In the old paradigm, surrender has been viewed as a sacrifice, as having to let go of something that you want or need in order to receive something later on down the line.

But this is an energetic vibration of lack and is part of the indoctrination of the third dimension, the dualistic matrix.

True surrender is trust in God; remembering that there is a great force that keeps our heart beating, and turns an acorn into an oak tree.

When we surrender, we are surrendering to the force that keeps our kidneys working, keeps our hearts pumping, keeps our lungs working. The force of creation – the in-breath and the out-breath combined.

Surrender is dancing in the knowing of Remembrance, that God holds you in every single moment, and every moment of your reality is perfect. Whatever is occurring, there is perfection in that divine plan, and it is teaching you aspects of yourself that are wanting to be healed and restored.

So please take these words as a sacred invitation to open your heart to all aspects of your divine self, remembering that your innocence must be claimed by you. The world will not grant you the mantle of recognition of your innocence, that is your birthright. For you are a sovereign being, and you would not want it to be granted to you from outside of yourself. That would completely and absolutely defeat the entire process.

So give thanks for this great sovereign Universe that we live in and understand that if you are waiting for an invitation to take full sovereignty of your divine self, this is it!!

Whether you accept the truth of who you are or not, the truth remains and all those with eyes that are awake see the eternal divine child self that dances in your eyes in all moments, in all days, and in all ways.

CHAPTER 16

Woman Leads

When I entered into my last relationship, I remembered many important ancient truths that being incarnated into the third-dimensional matrix had programmed me to forget.

With all the work that I had done on myself and all the enlightenment, awakenings, and expansions that I had experienced within my soul consciousness, I was very blessed when I entered into my last relationship to experience the living reality of the true role of the Divine Feminine, particularly in the area of sexuality and sexual merging.

It became apparent to me that my partner and I were experiencing PTSD on a sexual level from being incarnated into the matrix. With the bombardment of so many base sexualised images and programming from such a young age, this had led us to experience unhealed PTSD around our sexuality.

I remembered that patriarchal programming had entrained everyone to believe that it was the role of the Divine Masculine to lead the Divine Feminine in terms of sacred sexuality and the invitation to merge sexually. But as with all patriarchal programming, I remembered that this was a truth that was indeed flipped.

In my encounter with this relationship, I was brought to the realisation that I had done a huge amount of healing as the Divine Feminine, which put me at a level to be able to fully hold space for my beloved, in order to assist him to heal from his trauma.

In all of these revelations, it became apparent to me that it was indeed my role to lead him into the bedroom, also known as the healing sexuality chamber.

I remembered that it was my role to lead him sexually. I let go of the programming within me that was waiting for him to initiate our merge, and I realised that in the ancient temples of Isis, it was the Divine Feminine who was trained to heal, atone, and nurture the Divine Masculine sexually in order to assist him to go through the essential initiations from boyhood to becoming a fully-fledged man, and thus a fully-fledged Christed being.

I had reached a level of wholeness and healing within my own spiritual journey, so within this relationship, I was able to decipher the true spiritual codes that my higher self wished to reveal to me around the true dynamics of the role of the Divine Feminine in terms of leading the Divine Masculine into the temple of healing and atonement.

That relationship was an extremely powerful blessing for me, and it gave me the opportunity to walk my talk and have a direct experience of being a tantric priestess, working with the energies of the Isis temples, and fulfill the deep, sacred work of leading my Divine Masculine back to his original sexual innocence.

I received many downloads from my higher-self team on how to initiate this process, I am working on bringing through a programme that will enable you, who are reading this book to activate those codes and powerful initiations, that you may lead your partner back home to his original sexual innocence.

My higher self showed me the exact methods that I could utilise in order to create the circumstances for my beloved to absolutely, completely heal himself of all sexual dis-ease.

This beloved turned up in my life with a huge amount of sexual disease, as well as mental disease. It was my absolute honour to hold space for his miraculous healing, by inviting him into the sacred sexuality temple, so that he could receive the nectar of healing and atonement, which can only be initiated through the divine awakened feminine who has fully done the work, to heal, restore and atone her own sexuality back to its original innocence template.

It was through my own perception and recognition of him as an innocent son of God; as a Christed soul, that enabled him to activate those codes of Remembrance within his own consciousness, and thus truly begin his sexuality healing journey.

It was very liberating and aligning to remember the truth of my role as the Divine Feminine, as the priestess, as the healer, and my team made it clear to me that my job was to bring him to a level of profound wellness and healing. He would then have the skills to be able to hold space for me to clear any last residues of PTSD that were stored in my ancestral field, awaiting the moment of true and pure love, in order to be purged once and for all from my energetic system.

Somehow there was an unconscious agreement between us that I would hold space for his healing, and then once he was healed, he would hold space for my healing.

It was an incredibly life-changing experience being in that relationship. All the codes that I accessed and remembered were shared prolifically with my community, and many of us let go of a huge amount of patriarchal programming around the role of the Divine Feminine with regards to sexual leadership.

This is a huge subject matter, and I am so delighted that we have this space to be able to discuss this. Again, I highly recommend reading my book *Twin Flames & The Event* as it will give you a core foundational understanding of the teachings from which everything that I am sharing originates.

What I fully recalled and embodied is that the role of the Divine Feminine is to remember her innocence as a daughter of God. Through her own rebirth, she then activates her own feminine Christed Self and is indeed reborn as the feminine Christ. It is then through the purification of her vision and her perception, that when her beloved stands before her, she is able to recognise the divine masculine Christed self in him, as a mirror of her divine feminine Christed self.

Through this recognition and Remembrance, the seed of the Christed self within the Divine Masculine transforms to become the fruit of the Christed Self.

This is an alchemical process that has been hidden from humanity, and nearly all modern religions have sought to eradicate the true role of the Divine Feminine, with regards to the activation of the enlightenment and ascension of the Divine Masculine's consciousness.

However, the age of darkness is no more, hence these words are coming forth now in prolific glory and the promise of lasting transformation.

Dearest Divine Feminine, a message to you from my heart. The Divine Masculine is waiting for you. He is waiting to take your hand, for you to lead him home to the temples of innocence and sacred sexuality. He has been through so much trauma. He has been through so much abuse. His consciousness has been utterly polluted to levels that are unfathomable to you. He is in dire need of atonement and healing. You, through your own heart connections and womb portal, have not received quite the extent of brutal sexual programming as the Divine Masculine, and therefore it is your duty to stand up now as the leader, and meet him your brother, in full recognition of the innocence of his true nature.

There is no more waiting, Divine Feminine. This book is the message from your higher self, that the time for waiting is no more. The time is now. You are the leader. You are the leader in your intimate relationships. It is your duty to walk your Divine Masculine home back to his original innocence. It is your duty to meet him in the sacred depths of the temple of divine innocence, that you may merge in that blissful, playful, childlike way that Mother-Father God intended, so that all of the dross and horrific programming may be cleansed entirely and perpetually from both of your systems forever and ever.

CHAPTER 17

Connecting With Your Womb

On my journey of sacred sexuality and healing, I have done a huge amount of work connecting with my womb. During my womb connection prior to this profound healing work, I encountered very deep imprints of trauma that were stored within the womb area of my body.

I realised that this wasn't necessarily to do with experiences from this lifetime. The wounds were much more related to my ancestral lineage, and the abuse that had taken place within my ancestral line.

I have come to realise that as the first truly conscious, awakened one in my family lineage, I have somehow been given the huge task and responsibility to face the enormous destruction, toxicity, and poisoning of the sacred womb space, of my entire ancestral lineage. Essentially this means having to face a huge amount of violation that has taken place in that area.

In meditation, I encountered the true vibratory frequency of my womb.

I encountered her scars, and I encountered her grace. I encountered her resilience and her ability to be able to still keep showing up as the portal of wisdom, divinity and divine motherly service, regardless of the unprecedented amount of trauma and violation that she had experienced individually and collectively.

I spoke to my womb and she spoke back to me of deep pain, sadness and trauma due to her voice being silenced over many centuries.

The silencing of her voice made her powerless to protect herself sexually, which resulted in a huge amount of violation.

My womb spoke, and I cried deep tears for all my ancestors who were not awakened, who had experienced the intense trauma of being violated. I sat and I prayed at my altar.

I lit a candle and I visualised light pouring into my womb, into the dark places where the violations had taken place. I visualised light pouring in and filling up my womb space with warmth and healing grace.

I spent days and weeks filling up my womb with so much light, and I sent that light into her deepest crevices and caverns. And as the light entered, I became aware of all the programming that had become embedded into my womb, into my vulva, and into my genital area.

Programming around submission, programming around denial, a programme around shame, a programme around hiding. But the most destructive programme of all was the one that hid the truth of our innocence as sexual beings of divine love.

I surrendered and allowed the light to fill up my womb space, and I did a huge amount of work with my own Kundalini energy and experienced the Hieros Gamos: the inner alchemical merge of my own, inner masculine and feminine serpents that reside at the base of my spine.

Through that great work, which is known as the magnum opus, I was able to activate codes of profound, sacred union and Remembrance of the true blueprint that my womb space held beyond the wounding and distortions.

Thus, as the light continued to pour into my womb, I remembered that my true eternal divine beloved had been designated by Mother-Father God to be the guardian of my inner womb space.

I was extremely blessed to be able to meet him in meditation through the portal of my imagination, which is the gateway to the higher dimensional realms of consciousness.

Upon that high and deeply spiritual meeting and merge, I understood implicitly that my beloved resides within that womb temple space and within my own being.

I was shown clearly that my beloved is the guardian of the altar of my womb, and he is working with me on a profoundly deep level to heal all the ancestral wounds of sexual violation, rape and trauma that we, as a collective have experienced.

This is a huge subject, and please know that I've bought through a meditation, which can be accessed in the accompanying workbook. This meditation will enable you to directly visit your womb area and experience the pouring in of divine light. For more information and how to order, please see the resources pages at the back of this book.

My womb space spoke to me and requested more connection, more conscious touch, more communication on all levels. She asked not to be ignored. She asked to be touched in a way that is healing, in a way that does not wish to take from her, in a way that wishes to give to her.

As my womb space healed and I returned back to my original innocence template, it was an extremely explicit experience to behold, as I felt like all the codes that I was born with from my childhood reemerged and were reimprinting on my womb, energetically trumping all traumatic memories and timelines that I was clearing.

This is, of course, an ongoing process, and I continue to draw light into my womb regularly, and I'm so grateful to be writing these words and sharing this with you all. Reminding us all that it is so essential to fill up our womb space with light, and connect with our womb space regularly, in order to understand and fully resolve the traumatic wounds that she may be carrying.

A message for the divine masculines who are reading this book. You also have an etheric womb space that is connected to your mothers and all your grandmothers, and all the lifetimes that you have incarnated as a woman. It is highly appropriate for you to work on an etheric and energetic level with regards to healing your etheric womb space.

The divine feminine has been granted the extraordinary privilege of being able to birth souls from the unseen realms to the seen realms. She is the interdimensional portal that God has granted and ordained with the highest responsibility in the Universe, to guard over God's most precious creation: You, beloved children of love.

Therefore, the womb space points directly to the truth of the role of the Divine Feminine in the great grand scheme of creation, and her absolute fundamental priority and glory, being the portal that all life is born through.

CHAPTER 18

Decoding the Mysteries of the Masculine and Feminine Union

I hope that reading these words awakens you from any patriarchal spells that you may have been under, that have sought to deny and indoctrinate you away from the role of the true Divine Feminine, the mother of all creation, the one whom God has given the extraordinary privilege, to be the gateway for all souls reincarnating into this dimensional realm.

There is a reason that Mother-Father God has chosen the Divine Feminine to be the portal for souls to enter into this dimension, and that is because the Divine Feminine is deemed less corruptible than the Divine Masculine.

All this is depicted in the tarot. The zero card represents the Fool and represents the zero-point field; the sacred space from which all souls are born and die.

The first card is the Magician, which represents the Divine Masculine. The card depicts an image of the Divine Masculine holding his staff up to the sky, representing the fact that he is a channel and a conduit of divine wisdom and grace.

The second card in the tarot is the High Priestess. She is seen holding the book of knowledge, which is symbolic of the fact that Mother-Father God has deemed her less corruptible than the Divine Masculine with regards to being the gatekeeper for all souls, and the one deemed most responsible to hold the knowledge about the true nature of reality.

This truth is also depicted within the symbology of the story of Adam and Eve, whereby Eve eats of the apple from the tree of knowledge. Of course, patriarchy has massively distorted this story, but the true undistorted version is that Mother-Father God created it such that Eve was given more responsibility than Adam, therefore, she was allowed to eat of the fruit of the tree of knowledge, and truly understand the nature of reality, and be a portal to the souls that are birthing from the unseen realms into the seen realms.

There is so much to speak about on this subject, and because women are deemed to be so powerful spiritually, this is why I believe the important role of women in the evolution of humanity has been eradicated from the modern-day scriptures.

In removing this truth and sacred information, humanity has been robbed of its true power. Because, in truth, we can never access our true power in the face of lies.

We all hold the masculine and feminine energies within us. In truth, we are a balance of the masculine and feminine energies, and as we arrive at the vibrational plateau of spiritual mastery, we attain an extraordinary level of balance within our own masculine and feminine energies.

These energies truly reside within all of us. Therefore, the Divine Feminine and the Divine Mother reside within all men and women.

The Divine Feminine must be honoured and revered as the Mother of all creation, and as the one that Mother-Father God has deemed responsible to be the portal for souls to be birthed through, and the keeper of the gnosis about the true nature of reality.

So much has been hidden from humanity with regards to the role of the Divine Feminine. But if you search within all ancient mythical writings, even Christian mythological writings and Arthurian writings, you will find the true codes of this information are retained.

Also, within the Gospel of Thomas, you will find there are some codes that are still retained pertaining to the true role of the Divine Feminine. But please understand that her role was eradicated from the Scriptures in order to fully deny humanity of its true birthright, that being the truth of creation and the role of the Divine Feminine within that.

CHAPTER 19

Menstruation

Yesterday, I took part in a Divine Feminine round table with some beautiful, powerful and enlightened goddesses. The subject matter of the round table was menstrual cycles and how our menstrual cycles have been affected during the recent energies.

Every single one of us shared that we had experienced period anomalies within the last 12 to 24 months. A few of us stated that we were experiencing irregular periods and some of us had experienced our periods stopping entirely.

The information that I'm about to share must not be viewed as absolute. I am sharing a discussion that took place between myself and some highly awakened women.

As with all the information that is presented here, please take what resonates and disregard the rest. It is very important that you always stay aligned and at one with your own inner compass of truth. If something does not feel true for you then follow your intuition.

So bearing this in mind, I would like to share with you all what we discussed.

The predominant insight was that it seems as though our womb space is evolving from a lower density to a higher density.

We discussed how Gaia's desire to receive our sacred menstrual blood has been inverted and replaced by the man-made practice of bloodshed and war.

For many thousands of years, human blood has been used for malevolent and sacrificial purposes. In our discussion, we observed that we felt like this paradigm was collapsing before our very eyes, and as part of the ending of this cycle, we discussed the fact that it looks as though the current upgrades are being heavily targeted at the female womb area.

We shared that it feels like we are on a current trajectory whereby the womb space is being transformed and upgraded from a reality where collectively we shed blood once a month (as we release an egg from our ovaries) to a template of more immaculate ovulation, resulting in, one would imagine, an immaculate conception.

It is my understanding that this element of our genealogy and gynaecology was targeted specifically at the time of Atlantis when our DNA was manipulated and instructed to come out of its 12-strand diamond perfection formation into its current two-stranded scrambled formation.

Please see my book *Twin flames & The Event* where I discuss this in extraordinary detail.

In this manipulation, it would seem that the womb space was targeted to ensure that every month, the feminine physical body would shed the lining of the womb.

In our round table discussion, we talked about the time of Atlantis and Lemuria whereby we held memories of not bleeding as Divine

Feminines, and we shared memories of how that changed after the fall of Atlantis.

We all remembered that at that time we suddenly had menstrual cycles that were often extremely painful.

I now wonder if part of the reason why women's menstrual cycles were targeted at the time of Atlantis was to do with the fact that if women were afflicted with pain and discomfort once a month, this would massively affect their spiritual vibration and prevent them from harnessing their full spiritual power and radiating their full spiritual potential.

This could definitely be one of the reasons why women's menstrual cycles were targeted at the time of Atlantis.

In our discussion, we also spoke about the current so-called vaccination programme that is being inflicted upon humanity.

After reading a huge amount of collected research and evidence, it is apparent that the current obsessive vaccination programme is specifically targeting fertility and menstrual cycles. As a direct result many women are now having miscarriages, ectopic pregnancies, problems with their periods, completely irregular cycles, and are experiencing all sorts of anomalies taking place in their current menstrual cycles.

According to research, this is not only affecting people that have been vaccinated, but also affecting people that spend time around those vaccinated.

Much research is currently being conducted on this particular subject, but from what I can ascertain, people that have received the recent vaccine are shedding what is referred to as 'spike proteins', which are interacting with the hormonal set point within one's being.

In addition, these spike proteins are specifically targeting women's fertility and many people are experiencing spontaneous bleeding from various orifices when they are around those vaccinated.

In the next chapter, I will share more about the downloads I have received about how women's menstrual cycles are transforming and upgrading during these unprecedented times.

I would highly recommend that you place attention on your womb space, and work with healing frequencies that will harmonise your hormonal levels within your body.

I also highly recommend working with crystals that will support you hormonally, and I recommend taking supplements such as evening primrose oil and high-grade iodine. These supplements will massively support you to find equilibrium in your hormonal cycle.

CHAPTER 20

The Times We Are Living In

We are currently in the midst of a spiritual war. Yet the trickiest aspect of this fact is that 80% of the population remains unaware, and are just trying to get on with life, despite the constant attacks that the old powers that 'were' are inflicting upon humanity.

I would like to take this opportunity to remind everyone reading these words that we are never a victim, and even though we are in a spiritual war, we are experiencing a battle of frequencies.

Therefore it is absolutely imperative that you take responsibility for maintaining and managing your spiritual vibration.

The matrix would have you believe that you need to be dependent on external tools and devices, but the truth is your own DNA is a communication device of the highest order, which is waiting to be programmed by you.

If you do not programme your DNA, the despicable powers that 'were' will do that through the programming and disinformation of the matrix.

So please understand that within you exists the highest and most advanced technology in the Universe, and the Deep State knows this, which is why they try to keep everyone consumed with superficiality, consumerism competition and war.

It would serve you well as you read these words to fully protect yourself with the armour of God every time you go out.

We do this by speaking to our DNA.

Please take this moment now to ask your DNA to oscillate at a frequency whereby it is unaffected by EMF radiation warfare. Please see the resources section at the back of the book. where you can access a very powerful 21-day meditation programme to assist you to harness your DNA at a level whereby it is absolutely completely unaffected by EMF warfare radiation.

There are so many tools available that will enable you to fully stand in your sovereignty at these times of great transformation on our planet, as we bear witness to the collapsing of the old Earth.

There are many programmes, meditations, mentors, and guides that you can work with that will assist you on an extremely deep level to stabilise your frequency at a high and optimum level. As such, you will be able to stand as an illuminated beacon of perpetual light, unaffected by any of the frequency attacks that are taking place in any dimensional realm of consciousness.

No one is a victim on a spiritual level. We all knew exactly what we were signing up for when we decided to return back to the earthly plane at this time.

We are in the era of a great planetary shift and as far as I can ascertain we are all being tested to see whether we are sovereign beings or whether we are slaves.

There is no judgment. You are either a sovereign being or you are adhering to the timeline of slavery. Those who are adhering to the timeline of slavery will probably not make it in this ascension cycle, since in order to be able to fully harness the intense ascension energies that are now pouring into Gaia we all need to stand as illuminated powerful pillars of sovereignty and light, unmoving, and unbending. And most importantly never seeking approval from any external force other than God, our eternal creator.

Only those of us who are able to stand tall, and are able and willing to accept disapproval from any angle, are going to make it in this current ascension cycle. And again, please read my book *Twin Flames & The Event* where I speak in great depth about this current ascension cycle.

If you choose not to ascend in this current Ascension cycle, please know another cycle will come along soon and those that didn't make it this time can ascend on the next one.

If you are reading these words, no doubt you are either a first- or second-waver and I highly recommend working with all the teachings and tools outlined in this sacred book in order to assist you to fully step into spiritual mastery. Not only for you, but for all your brothers and sisters throughout all timelines and all dimensions.

CHAPTER 21

More on Menstruation

I would like to devote this chapter to exploring in more detail the subject of why so many women are currently experiencing anomalies in their menstrual cycle.

The information in this chapter is based on a poll that I ran in my Facebook group: 'The event is happening' where I asked them to tick the box that was most applicable to their situation:

1. I'm having slight anomalies with my menstrual cycle.

2. I'm having severe anomalies with my menstrual cycle.

3. I'm having no anomalies with my menstrual cycle.

Out of the 350 people who responded to the poll, around 180 women said they were experiencing slight problems, 150 said they were experiencing severe anomalies. While the remainder said that they were experiencing no anomalies.

The figures from this poll clearly indicate that something is fundamentally changing women's menstrual cycles right now.

After gathering that information, I meditated very deeply, contacted my spiritual ascension team, and asked them to share with me some important insights as to why they believed these anomalies were occurring in so many women's menstrual cycles. This is what my team shared with me:

Many women's wombs are going through a profound cleansing and purging at the moment, specifically related to the lifetimes in which they have experienced sexual abuse.

I have noticed in this current time period of observing menstrual anomalies, that quite a lot of women seem to be bleeding twice a month.

Whenever I tune into the reasons why this may be the case, I am flooded with insights that this is connected to a deep cleansing that is going on within the collective womb space.

It feels like the cleansing is so transformative within our womb, and the current purging energies are going deeply into the vibrational womb space of as far back as our great, great, great, great, great grandmothers who were abused.

The next insight that I would like to share with you all is connected to what I've been shown regarding an upgrade of the endocrine system, which is the system that governs our hormones.

My team showed me that in the recent past, the endocrine system has been operating on what could be described as a low vibrational current, connected to the vibration of our 3D carbon body. However, as we transform into our crystalline forms, the density of our endocrine systems is also adjusting and is moving out of its fixed state, into a more fluid state, as we transform from carbon to crystalline. Please see my book *Twin Flames & The Event* where I speak about this in detail.

We are in this process whereby we are shifting from third-dimensional beings into the awakening and Remembrance that we are multi-dimensional avatar beings. And so as we are transitioning from our 3D carbon forms to our 5D crystalline forms, it feels like our endocrine system is also receiving the necessary information to uplevel and upgrade itself.

Our endocrine system has been entirely calibrated and orientated to the third-dimensional system, but it feels like the current energies are shifting us and loosening up that rigidity that has held many of our cycles in place, and calibrated to a regular 28-day cycle.

So much density in our consciousness is shifting, and our bodies are shifting in order to align with the new vibrational templates.

I feel like part of the reason why many women are having these anomalies with their cycle is to transform and shake up the rigidity of how we've all been operating as third-dimensional beings.

Our bodies are transitioning from carbon-based to crystalline, and because of this, it is looking like our bodies are transcending their need to bleed monthly.

It also feels like the shift and transformation that is taking place is related to us transitioning to a species that no longer needs to menstruate.

I believe this is connected to the fact that this is all part of the 3D programming and the rigid vibrational template which has decreed that humans have a lifespan of around 80 to 90 years.

The aging programme that has decreed that human beings live a short lifespan is a huge distortion and inversion that was allowed to be implemented into humanity's consciousness at the time of Atlantis. However, nothing could be further from the truth.

Our physical vessels were designed for us to coexist in for as long as we desire. And they were designed for us to very, very consciously and naturally ascend at the moment of our soul's choosing.

As we anchor into our crystalline forms, we will be able to procreate much, much longer than this limited period of age 20 to 50, or whatever it is now. We are going to be able to reproduce at any time within our evolutionary cycle.

So many things are changing for us in this monumental Great Awakening lifetime. Old structures are collapsing, and new structures are forming that are in alignment with the truth of who we are as eternal crystalline beings.

I believe as we fully transition into our crystalline forms, we are going to transcend our body's pattern of bleeding monthly.

CHAPTER 22

Offering Our Sacred Blood to the Earth

Another area of importance that I would like to discuss in this chapter has to do with a very powerful reminder coming from our galactic star family: that it is very important for Divine Feminines to offer their sacred blood to the earth.

I went into a deep meditation recently, and I was shown very clearly that Mother Earth Is thirsty for our menstrual blood.

We, the Divine Feminine, are literally the Physical aspect of Mother Earth's body.

Our bodies are of the earth, the body of Mother Earth. And I was shown that she craves our nectar and the fluids: the sacred, holy fluids that are alchemically created in our sacred vessels and course throughout our systems.

A deep universal, primal reminder for women to collectively offer their blood to the earth, feels connected to the reason why so many women are experiencing anomalies with their cycles at the moment.

These anomalies are possibly a way of triggering us to change our relationship to our blood and the way we dispense our blood.

It feels like we are being invited to co-create a new relationship with our blood and the way we offer it to the earth.

I was shown that menstruation blood holds a particular geometric patterning that is linked to the perfect template of creation. So when we offer our menstrual blood to the earth it receives the interface of a perfect geometrical light grid, which enables her to release excess any trauma from her core that has been experienced due to bloodshed and war.

This feels like a very, very deep subject, and I really do not claim to have penetrated all the mysteries of this by any stretch of the imagination. I feel like I am literally skimming the surface of this huge subject matter.

I feel on a very deep intuitive level that the releasing of our blood is directly connected to the stargates of the Earth, and to the sacred sites of the Earth.

It is my intuitive understanding that it is very powerful for us to offer our blood to sacred sites in an intentional and ceremonial way.

I believe that our blood is also connected to the vibration of the dragons and the ley lines of the Earth. So as we mix our blood with the Earth, somehow this creates an alchemy that is connected to the activation of the Earth's Kundalini energy.

I feel intuitively that there is a symbiotic relationship between our blood and earth that has been lost, and somehow our generation is being called to reclaim that, and to really celebrate that, while the body's requirement to bleed monthly is being phased out.

The question is: does the body need to have this regular menstrual cycle as we align with our crystalline forms?.

I went into very deep meditation to explore this subject matter and this is what I was shown:

Women's menstruation blood is very sacred to the earth. And when we add our blood to the earth, this brings great calm energy to the planet, which can settle conflict and war energy.

This is connected to all the trauma and bloodshed that man has inflicted upon the Earth. The Divine Feminine blood is an extremely exquisite nectar from the gods that is encrypted and encoded with geometrical waves and patterns, that I was shown symbiotically merges with the crystalline codes and indeed the entire mushroom network of the Earth grid.

This conscious releasing of our menstrual blood enables the Earth grid to receive calm and peaceful energy after so much trauma and PTSD, due to the atrocities that man has inflicted on the Earth and humanity, including an unprecedented amount of bloodshed, that Mother Earth has had to mop up.

While I was in meditation, I was shown that when we consciously and intentionally offer our blood to the Earth, it actually settles conflict within that grid point; within that particular area. And it settles any individual and personal war energy in that community.

I was shown that when women offer their menstruation blood to the earth, this works on a deep, unconscious level to neutralise and clear war imprints and war memories that are stored within the unconsciousness of the Earth.

May these sacred words inspire you to go out and offer your blood to the earth. Your sacred blood is the holiest nectar in creation to Mother Earth as it was created in the sacred factory that is you – the individualised holiest aspects of creation: the Divine daughter of God in physicalised form.

It is worth considering that whatever is going on collectively with women's cycles at the moment, is symbolic and indicative of a break-down of many old structures, enabling us to create new ways and new systems which are aligned with working with the Earth. Working consciously with our menstruation through connecting it with the sacred sites, offering it to the earth, and creating that symbiotic relationship.

CHAPTER 23

Transcending the Need for Other People's Approval

On this journey towards Self-mastery and Self-realisation, whereby we truly awaken to our true value and true worth, to the extent that we have set vigilant impenetrable boundaries, in order to honour and protect our eternal divine child self.

For us to get to this place of alignment, it is absolutely imperative that we commit to the path of transcending the need for other people's approval.

The way I resolved this issue was primarily through my spiritual awakening into full God-consciousness.

As I awakened to God-consciousness, I realised that it was my duty and my honour to be the best daughter that I could possibly be to Mother-Father God, at all times and in all ways.

Due to the fact that I was committed to this and knowing that Mother-Father God was observing me at all times, I resolved it in my mind, that sometimes actions that I would be guided to take would not be understood and not always approved of, by human beings who were not awakened to God-consciousness.

I remembered that many people have their own filters of wounding and projection, which prevents them from seeing clearly the truth of another's actions and the purity of another's intentions. Therefore, it was very easy for me to come to the resolution that I did not need other people's approval. All I really truly needed was God's approval.

It is important to note that I was not always at this level of consciousness. I was in my early forties when I truly and absolutely transcended the need for other people's approval.

I had to descend into a dark night of the soul and experience the loss of many relationships. I had to step into the archetype of the black sheep of the community and speak the words that no one dares to speak.

I became a fearless truth-teller, a matrix shaker, living out the role of the Magdalene. A true rebel speaking her truth relentlessly, regardless of the approval of anyone else.

This was my individual journey, and it was a very powerful initiation, as I had to experience the loss of many relationships. But in truth, it became glaringly apparent that these lost relationships were no longer serving my highest good.

The situation taught me that our relationships can be very much likened to a tree. And as we grow, we shed old leaves and new leaves grow in their place.

Those old leaves and old friendships that we shed as we up-level our spiritual vibration and step into our truth are all predestined to leave our life at the exact designated time, as decreed by ours and the other person's higher self.

Therefore, I feel very deeply that we must all find our own way to resolve this deep programme of the third dimension, which through my observations has been specifically targeted towards the Divine Masculine.

I have noticed there are so many men who are deeply entrapped in the need to not stand out around other men, and to always be aligned with the status quo around other men.

It is my understanding that the third-dimensional matrix programming has been extremely intense for the masculine, in terms of heavily indoctrinating this harrowing false belief of conformity.

The times that we are living in are showing us that not every soul that is currently incarnated is cut out for this ascension cycle, as in order to be able to surf the waves of this current ascension, one must be truly rebellious towards all aspects of the matrix.

We must be able to stand tall in our sovereignty, armed with the ability to be able to make unpopular decisions and the ability to stand alone if necessary.

This current Ascension timeline is for souls that have the wherewithal and the ability to demonstrate genuine backbone and steeliness in their consciousness.

There are many souls that are wishing to be controlled and are unwilling to do anything that would jeopardise their community's opinion of them. And what I have been shown recently is that these people that are enjoying being told what to do and who are enjoying being very much on this conformist timeline, will get to stay and enjoy this 3d realm.

Whereas those of us that are fully in our sovereignty and have transcended the need for other people's approval and have fully activated our innate leadership codes understand deeply that collectively we are experiencing what is known as a bifurcation timeline split.

I speak about this extensively in my book, *Twin Flames & The Event*, but it definitely bares mentioning here.

There is a huge shift taking place collectively at the moment. This book is being written at the time of May 2021, in the time of what is known as the Great Awakening.

Many of us who are truly awake are observing a clear bifurcation timeline split occurring.

Those that are considered awakened to the agenda of the deep state and the old powers, are energetically and vibrationally splitting at the moment from those that are asleep to the controlled agenda.

There are those that are awakened to divinity, to the understanding that every aspect of creation is dripping in sacredness and divinity, and there are those that are absolutely comatose to this fact and believe that this is a third dimensional, superficial realm where you live, you die and that's it.

This is a very simple and generalised explanation of the bifurcation timeline split, but I feel it is necessary to bring this discussion into this chapter of the book, as we speak about transcending the need for other people's approval.

May the words in this chapter inspire you to really look at the ways that you filter your truth, the ways that you dim your light, the ways that you hide your rawness in order to blend in or not be seen or be approved of.

These times require warriors to shine their lights as brightly as possible.

If you are drawn to this message, know that you are a warrior of light, and please take this as permission to relentlessly shine your light and speak your truth, regardless of how popular it is with other human beings. Remember, it is our duty to keep God happy at all times.

CHAPTER 24

Divine Feminine as the Spiritual Protector

In my journey of spiritual awakening, which I speak about in great depth in my book *Twin Flames & The Event*, I experienced the hieros gamos: the inner alchemical merge of the masculine and feminine serpents that reside at the base of my spine; my very own Kundalini energy.

As this occurred on the inner planes of consciousness, I experienced what the primary axiom of creation states: 'As it is within, so it is without'.

In the inner merge of my own internal Kundalini energy, the true identity and knowing of my Divine Masculine twin flame was revealed to me, and thus the inner became a reflection of the outer and the outer became a reflection of the inner. And at that moment, I experienced the inseparability of all internal phenomenon and external phenomenon.

As I was experiencing this full Kundalini sacred union and the ensuing ascension of my consciousness, one of the immediate revelations that was shown to me as the Divine Feminine was the promise I made to my Divine Masculine that I would take on the mantle of awakening first in the matrix. Awakening to union with God, union with self, and union with my beloved divine counterpart on the inner planes of consciousness.

I promised him that through my awakening and illumination, this would be a guiding light for him on the spiritual realms, and would enable his heart consciousness, (which is the GPS system that God has created and placed inside all our hearts to guide us back home) to find me and unite at the perfect divine time.

In my full Remembrance as the awakened Divine Feminine, I remembered it was my absolute duty to stand tall and offer the deepest and most steadfast protection on all planes of consciousness to him my Divine Masculine. I promised him that I would rise as the truly awakened feminine Christed self on the inner and higher dimensional realms of consciousness.

I clearly remember promising him that I would stand as his guardian and protector, and that I would be a guardian angel for him: a lasting and benevolent light that will always help him find his way home.

The Divine Masculine will always be able to find his way home to his true Divine Feminine, since the sacred memories of each other are stored permanently as remembrance codes, encrypted in our cells, in our DNA and in our heart's electromagnetic field.

Thus, on my journey of awakening and merging with all that is, I remembered on an individualised level that I had promised my Divine Masculine, that I would protect him on the spiritual level.

I promised him I would stand as an illuminated beacon on the higher realms and work with ascended Masters such as Saint Germain, Archangel Michael, Mother Mary, Kuan Yin and many other ascended beings to assist him to cleanse the trauma that he had contracted to take on during this lifetime.

I promised him that I would assist him in the Dreamtime, on the deepest inner planes of consciousness to find balance, joy and equilibrium again in this time of temporary separation.

So, therefore, when I say that the Divine Feminine is the spiritual protector of the Divine Masculine, I speak from an extremely personal and direct experience of what I've been shown by my own spiritual ascension team.

In my awakening to this, I was guided to many ancient teachings such as Egyptian wisdom and native American teachings, which fully and absolutely recognise the role of the Divine Feminine as the spiritual protector to the Divine Masculine on the inner planes and the higher dimensional planes of consciousness.

That is how truth is revealed to me. And as with all the messages that I share in this book and in all the books that I bring through, you are always in every moment invited to use your own discernment.

We all must use our own discernment to ascertain whether something resonates as true for us. And if it doesn't resonate as true for us, that is the absolute truth, and I absolutely honour that.

This is an endlessly fascinating subject. And writing this book is turning out to be a powerful, transformative and alchemical experience for me personally.

I am going through so many upgrades and purges as I bring through these messages, knowing that these words are going to be imprinted on the hearts and souls of so many of my soul sisters and brothers.

Enabling the million Lotus petals of the heart to open again in full Remembrance of the divine beauty that we all carry. This exquisite, unique, exceptional sweet beauty that has been endowed upon all of us by our benevolent creator.

Every word in this book is infused with the intention to trigger your DNA and the codes of sovereignty and holiness that reside within you. Codes that are stored safely within your heart and within your own pineal and pituitary glands.

This is the one heart speaking.

May you allow these words to bathe your heart and soul, and trigger the memories that you experienced as a child. For if you would like to make God happy, it is vitally important to remember to hold the innocence and emptiness of the consciousness of a child.

The child is able to show up in every single moment: present and able and willing to play and have fun and be in service.

When we can show up in this way without carrying the burden of our 'story' we will then truly make God do a happy dance. And that my dear brothers and sisters is the subject of one of my next books that will be coming to you all very, very soon.

The Divine Feminine is the rose. She is the one who in my direct experience and awakening, is the one who promised the Divine Masculine that she would remember the oath that they made together to re-unite on the physical plane, in this time of the turning of the great cycle as we transition from the Age of Pisces to the Age of Aquarius.

In this great 26,000-year cycle, we promised all beings that we would awaken and remember the truth that we are innocent daughters of

God, and that the world has endowed upon us a false illusionary projection designed to keep us entrapped in timelines that are low vibratory and unserving of our highest good.

The words on these pages are like explosions to our hearts, targeting all of that old programming, and reminding us all of who we are and how powerful we are.

So may you open your heart now to receive these words of Truth spoken from your higher self:

You are a daughter of the Most High Mother-Father God. You are innocent. You are here to serve your brothers and sisters, and you have come here to assist in the transformation of humanity at this time of the great awakening.

Most people who are drawn to my work are on the twin flame sacred union path. And if you are a Divine Feminine reading these words, please know that your Divine Masculine is waiting for you to truly, truly awaken and remember who you are. To remember that you are a rose. You are a sacred, divine, precious, eternal, beautiful flower. He wants you to know that you are worthy of devotion. You are worthy of grace. You are worthy of all this.

You are worthy of love. You are worthy of being recognised as God's most divine, holy, feminine daughter. Yet in order to be recognised you must own who you are and own your own recognition, through the Remembrance that your heart is the living master of your soul.

CHAPTER 25

Only the Heart Knows the Way

In order to awaken spiritually, you must listen very deeply at all times to the messages, the guidings and the promptings of your heart, as this is the powerful GPS system that God has created to steer us extremely quickly towards our heart's highest destiny.

The third-dimensional matrix programming has sought to belittle and hide the truth of the power and the necessity of the heart to guide one's journey while incarnated on the Earth plane. If you wish to ascertain the difference between one who is truly awakened and one who is asleep, notice that the one who is asleep is generally oriented towards believing that the temporary, egoic, monkey mind is the master of one's being, whereas the one who is awake knows absolutely and truly, that the extremely quiet voice of the heart is the true master of the soul.

I highly recommend that everyone reading these words dedicate themselves to finding practices in your daily life that will enable you to attune your frequency, so you can receive and decipher the subtle messages of your heart.

There are many powerful tools and practices available. I find writing is an extremely powerful way for me to activate swift transformation in my vibratory field, especially if old energy emerges that is calling to be transmuted.

I find as an awakened soul that using the instrument of pen and paper is an act of extraordinarily powerful magic, since it is a way of directly placing my consciousness on the physical page. Each time this happens, I feel energetically that mountains and platelets in the Earth have quite literally moved.

Another great tool I work with is listening to high vibrational music and surrounding myself with extremely beautiful, prayerful, sacred music of a 432 resonance. I find that surrounding myself in sacred music is like medicine for my heart and often brings me to cry deep tears of Remembrance of heaven and home.

I encourage you to find whatever way works for you to that enables you to be able to discern the messages of your heart from your head.

Each time you feel triggered; each time you feel annoyed with the way someone responds to you or reacts to you, this is your inner-child self, your heart-self saying, "This behaviour is unacceptable. I deserve more than this".

It is time now for the Divine Feminine to awaken from this dark, long spell of patriarchy, which has taught us all to belittle and undermine the important voice of the Divine Feminine that resides within all.

The intuitive feminine knowing resides within men and women, and women have chosen, for the most part, to actualise, embody and externalise the feminine form.

Please know that these words are an activation from your higher goddess self, your higher God-self, to remind you that enough is enough.

No more playing small. No more showing up in the world as one who will accept being treated in a way that is not always deeply loving, honouring, and respectful.

The world has not reached the level (at this time of writing in 2021), to give you full permission to show up as the goddess that you are.

The matrix has sought to keep everyone obsessed with their outer egoic shell and has utterly confused the entire collective through the excessive glamorisation of the external and superficial.

However, the truth is that the external is simply an outer shell, which houses the extraordinary spark of the eternal spirit, which is your true and eternal self.

May we all remember that we are here to transform from a 3D caterpillar to a 5D awakened butterfly, in full avatar consciousness.

But first you must take ownership of your own crown.

CHAPTER 26

Take Ownership of Your Crown

At the moment of one's reincarnation, every single child of God receives a crown that is placed safely in their etheric field. This is an automatic process that occurs for every child of God, and it marks the true heritage of the soul.

We are all one. There is no separation from God.

All souls derive from the sacred union of Mother-Father God. And thus, we all house within our etheric and akashic records, a crown that is awaiting the moment of our Remembrance, whereby we awaken from the illusion of waiting for someone else (who we deem to have greater spiritual authority than us), to give us our crown or place our crown upon our head.

Instead, we remember that being a sovereign child of the universe, it is our duty and only our duty to reach into the etheric and akashic records, in order to take our crown out of those higher realms and place it directly on our head.

At that moment, when we place our etheric crown ON OUR OWN head, we come to full recognition of ourselves as divine, holy daughters of Mother-Father God, also known as universal love.

As we place that crown on our high and holy head, we truly activate and actualise our sovereignty.

Our sovereignty codes are stored within our DNA memory banks. And once the crown is placed on the head, this sends messages through the heart and the electromagnetic circuitry system, informing the sovereignty codes to be fully activated within our own DNA configuration.

It is your duty to place your own crown upon your head and in doing so, you are creating a permission field at a deep unconscious level, for all your brothers and sisters to also activate this level of consciousness within their own psychic awareness.

Through giving yourself permission to own your worth, you remember your perpetual innocence. You unconsciously walk around as a beacon of warmth and magnetism, particularly to children and to animals who will immediately sense your godly vibrations.

So this is an invitation at this moment to stop waiting for any external authority, training, certificate or teacher to give you permission to take the crown out of your etheric aura.

Dearest Divine Feminines, you promised your twin flame that you would awaken and remember your power as a sovereign queen.

How does a Divine Feminine present herself to the world when she is proudly wearing her crown?

She leaves a trail of rainbows and spiritual glitter everywhere she goes.

She is an oasis of self-realisation, which is unconsciously acknowledged by all who come into contact with her. And this is received as deep replenishment and nourishment at soul level.

She unconsciously sends out a pulse that automatically gives everyone permission to drop all filters and simply be their true and brilliant selves.

We are extremely magnetic to all beings, particularly young children and animals.

We are loved by all.

We have fully activated the codes of spiritual mastery and 5D avatar consciousness, whereby we have awakened from the spell of waiting and have stepped into the timeline of leadership, empowerment, and sovereignty.

This is an absolute game changer, and at this point, one can truly say you are a caterpillar no more.

CHAPTER 27

My Personal Experience of Activating these Codes

I feel guided in this chapter to share an important story with you all that illustrates exactly what happened to me when I activated these codes of no more crumbs within my psychic energetic field.

There were many significant and symbolic events that aligned for me at that powerful time in my life, but without doubt the most striking memory I have occurred on the day that I facilitated my last in-person residential retreat in Glastonbury.

It was an all-women retreat. And on the morning of the last day, I woke up, went downstairs and lo and behold directly in front of me was a huge, fully grown black raven flying around my living room.

It was a very freaky experience having this wild bird flapping around inside my home, but I knew its appearance was deeply symbolic.

I couldn't get the raven to leave my home. And so I left to go to the retreat. And when I arrived, I asked one of the ladies who happened to be an expert with birds to go and release the bird back into the wild – which she did.

I meditated very deeply on the symbology of why the universe had sent me a black raven of all birds. Why did such a powerful, majestic and deeply symbolic bird find its way into my living room on the auspicious final day of my retreat?

After meditating for many hours on the reason for this, I heard very clearly my spiritual team say, "He is coming home". When I heard those words, they resonated very, very deeply in the core of my being.

After this experience, I was then guided to buy myself a statue of a raven. And when I brought the statue home, I was guided to place the raven on my mantlepiece between the goddess Isis and the statue of the Green Man that I had on my altar.

Fast forward one or two months, and I hosted my next retreat, which was called the *Sisterhood of the Rainbow Rose*. And during this retreat, we focused deeply and specifically on womb healing and sexuality atonement.

During the time we spent together in the group we went into each of our chakras, cleared them, and then we aligned each chakra point with a sacred site in Avalon.

We worked with the energy of the sacred rose to cleanse and purify all of our chakras, and at the end of the retreat, we were guided to bathe in the White Spring for a ceremonial purification.

As we arrived at the White Spring, we saw two Divine Masculines standing there in all their divine glory.

I was told by my spiritual team that 12 participants would fill up the places on my Rainbow Rose retreat. But the day before the event, two participants dropped out, yet spirit still guided me to buy 12 roses to give out to 12 participants.

Prior to our arrival at the White Spring, I gave out 10 of the roses to the 10 women on the course. And when we reached the White Spring and saw the two Divine Masculines standing as guardians and protectors at the entrance, I intuitively knew that these two brothers were sent by the universe as part of the container that I was working with.

And so I reached into my bag and took out the two remaining roses and gave them to these two Divine Masculines.

A few days later one of the brothers who was standing outside the White Spring, knocked on my door and wanted to connect with me. However, I wasn't available to connect with him. He then proceeded to knock on my door many times yet I simply wasn't ready for our meeting at that time.

One day I woke up from a dream, and in the dream we were hugging.

It was eight o'clock in the morning and he knocked on my door and I couldn't believe it.

I knew it was an incredible sign from the universe that I was meant to open my door and give him a chance. However, I still sent him on his way.

A few days later I received a strong intuitive message to reach out to him. So I contacted him and immediately he showed up at the cafe where I was with my friends.

That day we walked up to Glastonbury Tor and myself and this beautiful man ended up coming into sacred union that night at the top of the Tor.

On that initial first day of our merging, it was so powerful. I was placed in the role of being the one who the universe sent to recognise him as his true, eternal, divine innocent Christed self.

This was a very transformative experience for him. And as we fully merged, we went on an incredible journey of healing extremely deep issues within both of us.

The man that the universe sent was not my twin flame. On the day that he walked into my life we both recognised each other as sacred partners, but we both knew deeply and intuitively that we weren't each other's eternal ascension partners.

We recognised each other to be *preparatory* twins. And we understood that the universe had sent us to be with each other in order to prepare us to be with our ultimate ascension partners.

I, myself, had not been in a relationship for quite some years, and it made perfect sense that the universe would send a spectacular, glorious, divine, masculine to open up my heart and energetic field, and indeed my physical body, to receive the divine love that the universe had in store for me.

I think it's extremely pertinent to mention that there is no way on God's green earth I would have attracted this relationship, had I not up-levelled my relationship by no longer accepting crumbs in my romantic partnerships.

I entered into a relationship with someone who absolutely and truly recognised me as the Divine Feminine. His only desire was to serve me and to be completely devotional to me at all times.

He came into my life, held me, massaged me, was my best friend, looked after me, cooked for me, did all of the practical jobs around the house and absolutely stepped into the vibration of devotion in terms of his love towards me.

I stepped into my role of being the deeply grounded awakened Divine Feminine. And I felt that in our sacred Union, I held the role of the mighty oak tree, enabling him to wrap his wild masculine energy around the vast and grounded oak tree of my being.

In turn, this enabled him to find his sense of groundedness and earthiness in the world.

It was a mutual exchange, and a beautiful relationship and is deeply connected to the symbology of the raven. When the raven entered my house, I knew that it was a sign from the universe that my time of being alone romantically was coming to an end. And that indeed the wild divine masculine was coming home.

I had completed the necessary work on my own spiritual vibration to reach a place whereby I no longer accepted crumbs. I had arrived at the place whereby I would only accept a Divine Masculine who brought the energy of unconditional love and endless devotion towards me, the Divine Feminine.

This was an incredible relationship and was very significant for me on my evolutionary path.

Our soul contract was not to stay together forever. And at the correct time, the universe sent the necessary people, situations and circumstances to orchestrate our breakup. It was something that I didn't understand with my 3D mind as we were so in love, but there was a force that brought us together. A force which now was forcing us to part ways.

I knew that if I went against this force, I would suffer consequences. And therefore I had to accept the will of the universe, which was for us to split up.

It was my understanding that we were both being released in order to connect with higher vibrational partners. Unfortunately, when we split up my partner at the time was triggered into another episode of confusion and depression.

Despite breaking up and him going on his individual journey, it was an incredible relationship, which proved to me that I had absolutely activated the codes of self-love, self-worth, and Remembrance of my true value.

The fact that I had attracted such a high-calibre relationship, one that was infused with the vibration of devotion, proved to me that I had done the necessary work and made the necessary shifts within my own psychic field, and the universe proved this to me through the outer reflecting the inner.

CHAPTER 28

Role of the Masculine

On my spiritual journey of awakening from being a woman who was unconsciously calibrated to accepting crumbs in my romantic relationships, to a woman who firmly and vigilantly stated her boundaries for all to see, I learned a lot about the Divine Masculine.

I learned that many men are unconsciously waiting for women to transform their own relationship with their self-worth.

I learned that men deeply want to step into the role of carer and server of the Divine Feminine's needs. However, so much of the programming of the third dimension has instilled in many men a sense of entitlement, which I observed, obscured the innocent desires of their soul, which is to serve the Divine Feminine.

I believe that this entitlement which many men experience is connected to mothers and their relationship with their sons.

So much of the patriarchal programming agenda has sought to keep alive the paradigm of men so often being mollycoddled and overprotected by their mothers.

I have observed that in the home environment many males are conditioned to not assist with the day-to-day running of the home.

I observed this even in my own life. I grew up with my cousin as my sibling, and there was a two-year age gap between us.

As the two girls, we were given a huge amount of responsibility with the household chores. And I distinctly remember my mum never doubting my ability to perform complex household chores with great skill.

My cousin and I were given a huge amount of responsibility to maintain the house. And the most memorable job that we had was doing the weekly family washing.

It was the 1970's and we did not have a washing machine, so every week myself and my cousin used to have to go to the laundrette with two or three large black bag's worth of clothes.

We had to split them into coloured clothes and white clothes. Then we put them in the washing machine, followed by the dryer and then we had to bring all the clothes back home, clean and folded.

At the time we did this job, I was aged seven and my cousin was aged nine.

When my brother and my male cousin were born, I remember observing that they were not given any duties or responsibilities to assist in maintaining the upkeep of the house. I don't even once remember my mum asking my brother to do the washing up.

I reflected on this years later and I asked my mum why she didn't ever ask the boys to assist. And she simply said she didn't think they had the ability.

I think that this attitude applies to many mothers and has had a huge effect on men collectively.

My own direct experience is that my mother expected me to have a very high level of ability and expertise in terms of running a household, and because she expected me to always do it right, I never let her down. I always went above and beyond her expectations and excelled in every job that she gave me.

Her expectations of the boys in the house had a huge effect on them and their level of competence. I know that in my brother's case, her lack of expectations towards him had a huge effect on the man that he turned out to be and the way he showed up in the world.

I think this has had a huge effect on men, and generally speaking has led many of them to feel and act in an entitled way in this world.

If we look at many different cultures, it seems women carry out the brunt of menial work.

I think it's important that we have this conversation as we need to awaken from this societal programming. And we need to return to the truth that beyond the filters, beyond the programming, beyond the indoctrination and the belief in the inadequacy, the masculine energy deeply wishes to serve the feminine, and wishes to be guided by the divine awakened feminine.If only more women understood this!

Through my meditations, I have been shown that on a profoundly deep level, the Divine Masculine wishes to bask in the eternal presence of the awakened Divine Feminine.

I believe deeply that men are encoded to seek out and be attracted to the Divine Feminine in order to release the codes of God realisation that are stored within their own unconscious mind.

One of the primary ways for the Divine Masculine to find his true Divine Feminine is for her to fully activate the codes of spiritual mastery within her own being.

She must remember that she is a goddess, and she must devote her life to removing all false programming, which seeks to label her as anything less than a goddess.

Once the Divine Feminine awakens and becomes an embodiment of her true spiritual self, then this unconsciously sends out a pulse to her divine counterpart, her God-ordained divine Beloved, that she is ready to be found by him.

I have been shown that it is the role of the Divine Feminine to be the spiritual protector of the Divine Masculine.

According to my spiritual ascension team, many of the Divine Masculines did not wish to return back to the earthly plane. It was their Divine Feminine counterparts who promised them fervently and avidly that they would awaken in the matrix, and in their awakening, they would activate codes within their unconscious field, which would send out a pulse, informing him of her coordinates and whereabouts.

The Divine Masculine, once he steps out of his comatose state, unconsciously seeks out the awakened feminine, knowing that she is the mother and she is the lover, and she holds the keys to his ascension and his self-realisation.

Unconsciously, the awakened masculine knows that it is only through the perception of the Divine Feminine, that the seed of the Christed self within him is able to transform to become the fruit of the Christed being.

It is through the magnetism of the Divine Feminine that the ego dies and is reborn as the awakened Divine Masculine.

It is so important Divine Feminines who are reading these words, that you drop your focus on searching externally for your divine counterpart, and focus deeply and implicitly on sweetening your own nectar, becoming as juicy and magnetic and irresistible as you possibly can be.

You do that by stepping into self-mastery and understanding that the present moment is where the higher dimensional party is eternally taking place. The master orientates their consciousness towards the present moment and is aware that thoughts of the past and thoughts of the future can induce fear, paranoia, and anxiety.

The true master is eternally and perpetually coherent and aligned in the present moment.

May you take inspiration from these words dearest Divine Feminine, and may you know that your Divine Masculine is praying for you to awaken and step into your divine goddess glory so that you can assist in his rebirth, into becoming the true divine Christed being that Mother-Father God always intended him to be.

CHAPTER 29

Conscious Relationships

I would like to devote this chapter to speaking about what I've been shown with regards to the future of romantic relationships.

In the old paradigm, relationships were very insular and oriented towards both partners staring inwards at each other, usually with the other person being the centre and focus of the relationship. In the new paradigm relationship, the centre of the relationship is always Mother-Father-God.

I have been shown that the relationships that will last and be the most sustainable in the new Earth will have to be oriented towards service to God.

Each person must make a commitment to serve God and please God in every moment of their life, while the purpose of their spiritual partner is to support the other's devotion to God.

We must keep God at the centre of our relationship, and we must commit to finding consistent ways to keep God happy.

We do that by understanding that Mother-Father-God has sent this person to be in an intimate relationship with us. This is an opportunity for us to see this person with the eyes of God: to remember their eternal divinity, innocence and worthiness to receive love and all the fruits of the kingdom and queendom of Heaven.

In the new paradigm of relationships, God is placed at the centre of our relationship.

We stand as a couple with God firmly anchored in the centre of our relationship. As such, we deeply cherish each other's relationship with our eternal creator and ensure there is always space for that devotional relationship to be deepened.

In a new paradigm relationship, our primary purpose is to look outwards from the relationship, and seek all the ways that we can serve our brothers and sisters, as well as the collective, through being in a powerful God-centered, unified sacred relationship.

In the new paradigm relationship, we understand implicitly the concept of oneness and that we are all one.

When one attains enlightened consciousness, we realise that our beloved has been sent by Mother-Father-God to give us the opportunity to love God in her physical form.

In a new paradigm relationship, the focus is on soul growth and soul expansion, with the understanding that it is always appropriate to stay in that relationship until the arrival of another who offers our partner a higher vibrational soul-based connection.

It goes without saying that when you are in a twin flame connection, you have attained your highest vibratory soul-based connection. But if you are not in a twin flame relationship, say, for example, you are in a soulmate relationship, and your twin flame comes along, in the new paradigm relationship, it is appropriate to let go of the soulmate relationship in order to create a space for the twin flame relationship.

We must always remember that the Universe is supporting us to be united with our highest vibratory soulmates and twin flames.

When we are unified with extremely high-calibre soulmates and twin flames, this creates a win-win for the entire collective. This creates a win-win for everyone that we are in a relationship with, be that our children, our ex-partners, and our friendships.

The Universe always benefits when we create space for higher vibratory relationships to anchor into our reality, and when we are willing and able to let go of relationships, whenever this higher soul-based relationship enters our reality.

In the old paradigm, everyone was very attached to earthly commitments, regardless of whether or not they were serving the soul consciousness.

We cannot take this outdated attitude and thought-form into the new Earth.

In the new Earth, we must have an incredibly, powerfully anchored maturity that understands that we must always be willing to let go of partners if a more compatible partner aligns with our partner on a spiritual level. In doing so we understand that as we let go of that relationship we are clearing space for a much more compatible and higher soul-based union to anchor into our realities.

In a conscious relationship, we are completely open, honest, and authentic about who we are. We share openly our growth, our expansion, our blocks and our shadows.

In a new paradigm relationship, there is an understanding that our personal romantic relationships are a sacred opportunity for us to deeply restore and atone aspects of our shadow self. We will have the opportunity to share and release our shadow self while the other person deeply holds space for us, without any judgment, eternally recognising our innocence and perfection on a soul level.

When we view ourselves in this way, we massively accelerate the healing process which enables us to release deep, long-held trauma that has been stored in the cells, ancestral memory banks, and even Akashic records from past lives.

This is why it's so important for everyone reading these words to make a commitment to step into a conscious relationship and let go of being in an unconscious relationship.

An unconscious relationship is defined as a bed buddy and someone who you are joined with in order to support and look after you on a material level.

Very often, unconscious relationships can be referred to as karmic relationships. These are attracted into our reality when we haven't reached full enlightened consciousness, and we have bought into the timeline of lack. We attract karmic unconscious relationships as a mirror of our own consciousness and lack of awareness.

Most unconscious relationships are primarily based upon our programming and our wounds. For example, many people attract karmic relationships because they are afraid to face the reality of true love because true love makes you vulnerable to the actions of the other.

This is why people avoid high-level soul-based relationships, as so much is invested in these relationships. However, with a karmic relationship, hardly anything on a soul level is invested. Therefore, if that person was to leave you or abandon you, there is an unconscious understanding that this would not activate deep trauma within you, as it would if you were in a twin flame, soul-based conscious relationship.

I hope and pray that this chapter inspires you to ascertain whether you are in a karmic unconscious relationship, or whether you are in a conscious soul-based relationship.

May you take the words on this page as a sign from your higher self to inspire you to let go of any energies that are not serving your soul's deepest and grandest expansion.

When we hold onto these relationships, we block our true love from entering into our sacred space. A perfect analogy to describe this is if you imagine your life is like a theatrical performance. If you are in a karmic relationship, that person is acting as the hero or the heroine on the stage of your life.

You can imagine that your twin flame, perfect soulmate relationship is waiting in the wings, but this person will not enter onto the stage of your life until the other person exits.

So, therefore, see the words on this page as an invitation for you to find the courage to let go of any karmic unconscious relationship that is not primarily focused on service to God and devotion to the other through the understanding that Mother-Father-God has sent this person as an embodiment of the eternal God within and without for you to adore, serve and be devoted to throughout your lifetime.

There's much to speak about on this subject and I look forward to sharing more in even greater depth.

CHAPTER 30

⸻⸻⸻

The Future of Relationships

I would like to devote the next chapter to sharing how I see the future of relationships on planet Earth.

When I experienced the ascension of my consciousness in October 2013 and experienced the integration with my divine counterpart on the higher planes, I understood implicitly that my soul was preparing me on a very deep level, to be in an intimate relationship with this person, who had presented themselves as my twin flame on the inner planes of reality.

However, I also understood that it was a complex phenomenon, the coming together of two genuine bonafide twin flames, and I was aware that it may take a little time to manifest this relationship from the unseen to the seen realms.

My spiritual guidance team came forward and explained to me that the only way I could be in a relationship with another person other than my divine counterpart was if I was completely upfront and transparent about my connection with my twin flame.

My ascension team presented to me a vision of meeting someone and having a conversation with them along the lines of, " I am so deeply grateful that our paths have crossed and I know it is the will of the divine that we have met. But I need you to know that I know who my twin flame is, and I am destined to unite with him in this lifetime. However, we're not ready right now to come into physical union. So it is my understanding that the Universe has sent you as a preparatory partner to assist me and help me to become ready to unite with my true twin flame when its time.

There are many reasons why my team showed me this vision, and the main one I believe is to do with transparency, authenticity, and the knowledge that I could no way enter into a relationship and hide the truth about my eternal connection with my divine counterpart.

After some time of me experiencing the internal marriage between myself and my twin flame, the Universe sent me a beautiful Divine Masculine who was very deeply connected spiritually to my twin flame.

On the day that we got together, we both acknowledged that we were not each other's ascension partners, and we both acknowledged that the Universe had sent us to each other in order to prepare us for our forever partners.

It was so life-changing having this conversation with an awakened masculine, and his words to me were, "I promise you I will be the man to get you to your twin flame". I was blown away. I never imagined I would find a man who was able to hold such a stabilised level of emotional maturity. We remained committed to this knowing throughout our entire relationship.

I believe that this is the new paradigm for relationships. More and more people are waking up to the fact that their ascension partner has been chosen by Mother-Father God to assist them to ascend in the most efficient manner possible. The soul, therefore, is deeply programmed to unify with its ultimate ascension partner.

For some of us however, this can take a little longer to manifest on the physical plane.

I believe it is absolutely appropriate that we do not have to abstain from emotional and sexual connections with other people when we know who our true twin soul is, as long as we remain open and transparent about where our heart is truly oriented.

I believe that the future of relationships is all about transparency and authenticity. This includes the ability to have mature conversations, where we talk about the fact that we are either twin flame ascension partners or not.

If we are not twin flame ascension partners, it is imperative that we are able to hold space for each other to step into these relationships when they manifest in our physical reality.

What Mother-Father God showed me in my enlightenment experience is that it is extremely beneficial for the entire collective and the Universe at large, when genuine, bona fide twin flame ascension partners come into recognition and physical union with each other.

The energy and potency that is experienced between them is so powerful that it literally lifts the Earth out of the third dimension and places it into the fifth dimension.

What my team showed me is that the entire Universe and all souls are oriented towards fully supporting the highest ascension soul partners to come into physical union, as unconsciously, everyone knows that this frequency is the trump frequency. So the more people who come into these ascension partnerships and twin flame sacred relationships, the more the entire collective will benefit.

There is much to talk about on this subject and please know that it is my deepest honour to come forward and share with you my insights and inspirations around this matter.

I believe that we are currently experiencing an incredibly important rite of passage in terms of personal relationships, where we are transcending our selfish tendencies and coming home to a place of profound maturity and understanding.

We are maturing to a point whereby we are remembering that it is always appropriate to let go of a relationship if someone else comes along who can offer a higher vibration and connection than the person with whom we are currently in a relationship with.

The Universe is always supporting us to experience the highest vibratory relationships, and as we mature as a collective, more and more people will understand this and be extremely gracious when it comes to letting partners go when a higher vibratory partner comes forward.

This concept may seem outlandish to some, but while we were on the subject, I would like to share with you my opinion about polyamory. I believe that polyamory does not serve the soul consciousness, as it is my understanding that the soul deeply thrives on commitment, solidity and connection.

The soul consciousness can become very destabilised when the person that you are intimate with also shares intimacy with other people. This behaviour does not make the soul flourish, as the soul requires attention, focus, commitment and attentiveness to grow, and be able to expand in this challenging realm.

It is my understanding that many people choose the path of polyamory as a way to avoid intimacy because it is only truly when we are faced with a deeply committed relationship that we are able to do the shadow work that we have come here to do.

This means meeting, facing and alchemising all separate, wounded aspects of our shadow self as they get triggered and highlighted by our romantic partnerships.

If one is in a polyamorous relationship, the opportunity to do the extremely deep, focused work in a pristine and safe environment is extremely challenged. It is my understanding that this causes a delay in the soul's evolution, as the soul is perpetually programmed to thrive on commitment, stability, focus and attention. Of course, there is no judgment if you choose the path of polyamory. God is not judging you. No one is judging you. It is simply a choice and we must all make choices based upon whether they serve us and the collective.

If you are choosing the path of polyamory, I would invite you to look deeply into your childhood and explore any patterns of neglect, abandonment, or abuse that you may have experienced. It may be that your desire to experience polyamory is connected to your unconscious needs to perpetuate the timeline of separation that you experienced in your childhood.

Of course, as ever, this is an extremely deep and complex subject and I'm only skimming the surface here. But I hope that the words in this chapter have inspired you to look deeply at how you hold yourself in relationships, and at the level of openness and transparency that you are willing to share with your partner.

CHAPTER 31

Divine Feminine Speaks

Dearest Divine Feminine, it is not random or by chance that you are reading these words. You are reading these words because you are a spiritual leader and have made a soul contract to align with the codes and the frequencies on these pages. The sole purpose and intention of this book is to remind you that you are a sovereign queen of the highest order, yet the matrix has programmed you to believe that only an external authority outside of yourself has the ability to acknowledge you as the sovereign queen that you are.

This is an illusion. We live in a self-sovereign universe, and it is your duty to claim your own crown and place it on your head.

Please know that the Divine Masculine is waiting for you to awaken. He is waiting for you to become the spiritual master; to be the one who is able to be the observer of her monkey mind, to not be pulled and swayed by the temporary rise and fall of thoughts, emotions, and sensations.

When you have reached this level of stability and alignment, you send out codes and frequencies in your auric and akashic fields, which are directly received by the Divine Masculine that God has chosen to ascend with you in this lifetime.

The Divine Masculine is magnetised to the awakened, empowered sovereign woman, and deep in his soul and subconscious mind, he is praying every day and every night for her to manifest in his reality. For when she shows up in his reality, she stands as a beacon of illumination and goddess light.

She stands upright in her goddess power: unmovable and unshakable to all of life's challenges that are presented to her.

She is mother. She is daughter. She is lover. She is a child. She is the elder, and she is the galactic avatar goddess.

She is everything that your soul has ever prayed for.

The awakened goddess has recognised her egoic consciousness as the imposter and has understood that the heart consciousness reigns supreme on this journey through physical experience.

If you are graced with the presence of an awakened Divine Feminine, know that she will stand tall as the mirror, showing you all the places in your psyche that need to be atoned, and all the aspects of your psyche that need to be revealed, in order for you to harness your full spiritual power.

She will guide you lovingly towards your shadow aspect, showing you that the master embraces the shadow, and only the fool runs and hides from the shadow aspect. She will nurture you. She will stroke you. She will heal you with her powerful hands. She will hold you accountable in every area of your life and inspire you to show up as the glorious Divine Masculine that Mother-Father God intended you to be.

She will champion you, and be your best friend and greatest ally and support.

She will guide you in the ways to enable your dreams to come to fruition in the fastest and most efficient manner possible.

She will guard you and protect you on the spiritual level, particularly in the fourth-dimensional realm, where there is still a huge amount of duality and malevolent forces.

Know that she will work with the archangels and Mother Mary to be your spiritual protector on the inner planes of consciousness.

The Divine Feminine, who has done the work to fully harness her goddess codes, is a rare breed indeed. And if you are lucky to be in the presence of one, thank your lucky stars and thank all the angels and archangels for aligning you with this miracle of beauty and presence.

Conclusion

It has been extremely life-changing for me to bring forth this message for the collective, so I would love to know how your heart has received this book. And whether reading it has brought about any shifts and transformations in your consciousness, and in your reality. Please email me with any insights and awakenings you have received.

Every word in this book is encoded with a prayer that you may remember to stop waiting and start acting. Start acting like you are one who has fully claimed your sacred innocence and your sacred heritage.

Walk through the world as a queen or as a king, owning your inherent value and worth, so that everywhere you go, you intrinsically remember that you are worthy of the deepest honour, love and respect. And if you are treated in a way that is not in such alignment, then it is your duty to set extremely clear boundaries, in order to protect yourself and inform the Universe that such energy is not allowed into your field.

As you say "no" to the old energy, which may have played a part in your previous life, please know that you are opening the door to thousands of alternate timelines, whereby you will align with that which your heart has come here to deeply experience. This is an eternal sacred union and ultimate ascension with your twin flame, your God-mate, your best friend throughout eternity; your spiritual ascension partner.

There are so many names for this, but twin for me truly encapsulates the living experience that I am having with my current connection: that we are absolute twins, one in a feminine form, and one in a masculine form.

All of us on the ascension path, as we deeply immerse ourselves in oneness and marriage with God, have a direct and living experience of the primary axiom of creation which states, "As it is within, so it is without". And as we have a direct experience of living this, this ensures the absolute fulfilment of our destiny, which is to unite with our highest spiritual partner - throughout all timelines and dimensional realities in this lifetime.

The words in this book are here to remind you that it is your duty to set the standards as to how you are treated. And as you say "no" to that which you do not wish to experience, you are actually saying "yes" to that which you do.

The Universe always works in a very, very fast way when we align ourselves with God's great plan. So may you remember who you are, remember how sacred your blood is. Remember that you are a manifestation of the Divine Mother herself: perfectly imperfect, flawlessly flawed, but in God's eyes, perpetually perfect.

May you own your value. May you own your worth. May you set your boundaries. May you draw your red circle around you. May you never, ever accept crumbs. May you remember that prior to your incarnation, you and your divine counterpart sat at the feet of Mother-Father God, and you prepared every single aspect of your journey towards your physical reunion. And in that time when you were preparing for this inevitable union, your Divine Masculine came forward and said, "My darling, what I have for you could be the equivalent of the greatest Michelin-starred meal you could ever imagine. So please, please stop going to places where you can only get crumbs, because you'll never ever find me. Please remember you have to transform your own vibration in order to only allow energy that is recognising, honouring and ultimately that is devotional towards you, the Divine Feminine".

I remember clearly as I sat at the feet of Mother-Father God, myself and my divine counterpart made this promise to each other. I promised him that I would break the curse of all my ancestral lineages, which had directly experienced crumbs, upon crumbs, upon crumbs. And I will transcend that pattern through my own power, and recognition and Remembrance of who I truly am as God's eternal, innocent daughter.

I remember that conversation well, and I'm so grateful to my beloved for triggering that life-changing moment on the rainy streets of London, whereby I fully, absolutely awoke from the spell of believing that it was my duty to chase after a man and go looking and almost beg for scraps from a man.

Thanks to our soul agreement, I woke up from that spell and the momentum of that awakening is truly expressed in the words that are written in this book, in this empowerment manual for the Divine Feminine.

There are many exercises and meditations that will help you with this process. You will find them with the workbook that I have created that accompanies this book. I highly recommend working with the meditations and the exercises, as they will assist you on a deep alchemical level to embody and actualise your true value and worth.

As ever, it is my deepest honour to bring forth this sacred message to you all. I look forward to bringing through my next book, which could easily be called, *How to make God do a Happy Dance.* But let's see what the ascension team has in store for us. I love you all. **In love and eternal light, Jen**

PLEASE LEAVE A
REVIEW ON AMAZON
IF YOU HAVE ENJOYED THIS BOOK

It is my deepest and sincere prayer that this book has given you a profound understanding of the Divine Feminine and I hope you will find this book to be a valuable resource.

If you have enjoyed this book and found it helpful, please consider leaving a review on Amazon. Your reviews are hugely helpful to me as a published author and will help others be able to find this book in the Amazon search results.

Thank you, brothers and sisters, for all your support.

BOOK REVIEWS
NO MORE CRUMBS
AN EMPOWERMENT MANUAL
FOR THE DIVINE FEMININE

Just a note to thank you for including me in your street team and sending me the chapters to read.

I experienced sensations in the body, tingling in the solar plexus and womb area. I was emotional, tearful and started to feel tired. I realised my own vibration has been keeping me from manifesting what I'm worthy of and it's up to me to change it.

Sharon

From the opening paragraph I felt held and lifted, an expansion of my heart and activity in my third eye. Part of me was shouting yes! I re-

member and the words flowed into my consciousness, being and belong there. As I read on I recognised the truth of your words and the patterns of my relationships and here was guidance to co-create the reality of my desire. The wisdom shared illuminated a reinterpretation of events and a deeper understanding of who I/ We are. This book is a compass for all divine feminine to step into their power and navigate their lives. Thank you is insufficient for such an amazing gift of guidance.

Karen

Having just read the first 5 chapters I was so deeply moved by every word.

As I was reading, I felt like I was shedding so much conditioning and programming that this matrix has had on me/us... that I have been working through myself before, but your words just allowed these blocks to fall way!

After wards I went through a deep purge releasing all the areas. I had given my power away from being programmed and not feeling my true worth.

But this book just activates a remembrance of your true divine self.

Sarah

NO MORE CRUMBS
AN EMPOWERMENT MANUAL
FOR THE DIVINE FEMININE
WORKBOOK

Jen has written a workbook which is the perfect companion for this sacred text.

Halfway through writing this book I was very strongly guided by spirit to create a workbook that would accompany this powerful sacred scripture. So therefore, I followed this guidance and brought through an amazing offering that will assist you deeply to understand and assimilate all of the information and codes that are shared in this book.

I would highly recommend everybody work with the workbook, as the exercises and meditations work on a deeply subconscious level and work with the incredible power of symbols, which are **the** language of the unconscious mind.

If you really want to experience a shift in your vibrational reality and receive great assistance in truly becoming one with your higher self, then I highly recommend you gift yourself this beautiful workbook that goes alongside this sacred text.

I will now share with you a couple of preview chapters taken from No More Crumbs – An Empowerment Manual for the Divine Feminine Workbook.

No More Crumbs Workbook
Activating Your Crown of Sovereignty

As I have covered in a previous chapter, I would like to now devote the next few pages to speaking about the importance of activating the crown of sovereignty that exists within your etheric field.

Every time a soul is created, Mother-Father God places an etheric crown in our auric field, awaiting the moment of our remembrance, that we may reach into our auric field and take our crown out of the etheric and place it on our head.

This is a self-sovereign universe, and therefore there is no spiritual authority in the universe that has the power to give you your crown. Therefore, only you have been ordained with the spiritual authority to place your own crown on your own head.

As soon as you place your crown on your head, you are visible to other star beings who are also on this path of sacred sovereignty.

It is an act of profound generosity to awaken to this level and to unequivocally fearlessly wear your crown perched securely on your head.

Every time someone awakens out of the matrix to the remembrance of their true divine self, that Mother-Father God has given them a crown in their etheric field, this activates these codes to come online within the collective grid. This inspires many people to up-level their vibration to come to that realisation.

The role of the trailblazer can be likened to being stuck in a dense forest with no trails. The role of the trailblazer is to create the path and trail through the forest using all of the tools that we have at our disposal, which essentially will make the path much easier for all the other souls to move through.

This is what we are doing. We are trailblazing new paths in divine consciousness so that these codes are easily accessible by anyone who does the work to raise their vibration to this level.

To Purchase the No More Crumbs Workbook, please visit this link:

<u>No More Crumbs Workbook</u>

QR Codes to scan to access all of Jens Sacred Offerings are available at the back of this book.

No More Crumbs Workbook
Activating Your Crown of Sovereignty Exercises

Make a list of all qualities that you believe you will embody once you are fully wearing your crown of sovereignty, such as fearless communication, fearlessness around other people's disapproval, ability to shine relentlessly regardless of anyone else's opinion.

Write out all the ways that you intend to shine and be seen by your brothers and sisters as you wear your crown.

Please use a piece of paper and describe your crown in as much detail as possible. If you are artistically inclined, I would also encourage you to draw a picture of your crown using another sheet of artist paper.

Please note that I have bought through an extremely powerful meditation that accompanies this chapter.

I hope and pray you take deep inspiration from this chapter and go out of your way to connect with your own etheric crown and place it back on your head. I hope that you're inspired to go out and create your own crown or align with an actual physical crown that will remind you of your sacredness, divinity, holiness, and grace as a divine feminine daughter of God.

No More Crumbs Workbook
MP3 Activations

- Red Circle

- No More Story

- Hijacked Mind

- Christ Self

- Throat Chakra

- Crown Chakra

- Womb Healing

Working with the MP3 activations which accompany the No More Crumbs Workbook deeply and profoundly fast tracks your spiritual ascension path and enables you to activate these codes of transformation very swiftly and efficiently within your energetic system. I cannot recommend working with these activations highly enough.

No More Crumbs is also available as an Audiobook, please visit:

No More Crumbs Audiobook

TWIN FLAMES AND THE EVENT

Here is a preview chapter from Jens first book – Twin Flames and The Event.

Twin Flames and The Event
Preview Chapter - Prologue

Before me, I was shown a scene where I stood as a soul before Mother-Father God. In that scene, I could see that I had the choice of multiple different life paths ahead of me. They were displayed as mountain paths and peaks ranging in size and beauty.

I was shown that at that moment, where that choice was given, my soul very courageously stepped forward and said, "I choose to take the path with the highest peaks and the most exquisite vistas."

At this point, Mother-Father God came close and said... "My child, you truly are one of my most courageous beloved children, but I must forewarn you that this path that you choose is a most challenging one. As on this path, many times you will feel alone and abandoned by me. As all around you, you will see others who have taken the less high paths and things will seem easy for them.

"But my child, the one that you have chosen, is the one that delivers you back to your full ascended Union with your beloved Twin Flame. This will ensure the anchoring of the new paradigm of sacred relationship, deeply into the core of Mother Earth.

"Taking this path means that whenever you seek outside yourself for love, through relationships, substances, food - or any addictions, you will never find it. This is how I have created it to be. It is only by turning back to me, turning back to yourself, that you will ever find the solace, comfort and love that you seek.

"There will not be many people on Earth at this time who have chosen this path. You will be blazing a trail. You are one of the way-showers. This path will be very, very hard for your ego and you will feel angry at me when you can't manifest the love that you are seeking from outside of yourself…. Beloved child of my heart, are you sure you want to choose this path?"

And my soul in all her courage and bravery said, "Yes God, I choose that path, as taking that path will be my greatest service to humanity. That is my heart's intention: to serve humanity. The needs of my ego are insignificant to me," and God replied, "You say that now my child, but it won't feel like that. You can still opt for the easier path, whereby you will meet a soulmate early on in life and you will create an easy and comfortable life together.

"You will have some challenges, but at the end of your lifetime you will not have attained the spiritual insights and wisdom that the higher path will offer you, as you will not have had to face your shadow self, your ego or the void within you. Indeed, this easier path will prevent you from coming as deeply home to me, but it will be easy and comfortable."

"But God, how will I be able to come back to you? How will I know how to turn to you? Will you show me and guide me in the ways that I can truly turn back to you, as my saviour, my guide, my home, my sanctuary?"

"Yes, my child, I will be able to show you how to do that, as your connection with me will be so lucid and pristine, it will be easy for me to reveal that to you."

"So, tell me now God, how do I do that, how do I turn to you?

"My sweet, sweet child, your willingness to turn to me is 99% of it. Your willingness is symbolic of your failing at finding love outside of yourself, and when you have failed at that, you will turn back to me.

"There will be homesickness on your path, where you will cease to be gratified by external sources of love, and that will be deeply painful for you and your inner child - but remembering who I am, and your connection to me, is your salvation.

"You will remember that I have my arms eternally outstretched before you and am ever beckoning you back home to my heart, and your memory of that will bring you back to me.

"My precious child, your task on this Earth is to remember that you are seen and held, adored, comforted, protected and filled by me. As you remember that deeply, you will be carried up this seemingly treacherous path with great ease, and you will automatically attract your beloved from the space of alignment and divine perfection.

"The love that is your destiny is a direct reflection of the love I have for you. I love you beyond words, beyond sentiments, beyond ideas. When you know and rest in this love and truly deeply know it from the depths of your being, then and only then can it be reflected outside of yourself.

"You, my sweet child, are on track now to reach this most stunning vista that we have co-created together and it comes from all of this hard work and discipline that you have diligently committed to.

"Well done, my sweet, sweet child; I rejoice in your remembrance of my deep love for you, as you remember how your cup is filled and is overflowing, and that the deep void that is the hallmark of the ego self- is filled, not from a substance outside of itself, but from;

"I Am that I Am - God Source Within."

To Purchase the Twin Flames and the Event Book, please visit this link:

Twin Flames and The Event Book on Amazon

QR Codes to scan to access all of Jens Sacred Offerings are available at the back of this book.

Twin Flames and The Event Workbook
Preview Chapter - Working with your Inner Child

Inner child work is extremely important for those of us on the spiritual path. Unless you were born to completely enlightened parents, there is not a soul alive who is not suffering to some degree or another from PTSD (Post Traumatic Stress Syndrome), due to being born into this third-dimensional matrix.

We are all for the most part, brought up by adults who have no recollection of their spiritual heritage, the fact that we are all divine beings, having a temporary human experience.

Because of our care keepers' lack of spiritual knowledge, this has created a huge problem whereby many children have been bought up and have received deeply destructive programming.

As children, we do not have the consciousness to be able to unravel the trauma that happens to us. And so, oftentimes, what happens is that the trauma remains stuck in our energetic field. A perfect analogy to describe this process is a stuck record. If we do not process the trauma that we experience, as and when we experience it, then the trauma gets stuck and lodged into our etheric field and keeps going round and round.

Once this energy is stuck, this means that pranic energy, also known as chi energy, is unable to flow freely throughout the vessel. This is one of the by-products of not resolving your childhood trauma.

Another side effect is that very often you attract circumstances that will restimulate the original trauma, which you will experience in your life as a repeated pattern.

At some point on the spiritual path, you will become aware of your own beautiful, sacred inner child and you will remember that our soul consciousness is deeply connected to our eternal child self. And one day, maybe today you will remember that in the eyes of Mother-Father God, you will always be that sacred divine child.

At some point within our spiritual evolutionary journey, we realize that the child self is the most powerful and most potent aspect of our consciousness and we must do whatever it takes to connect with our inner child and make them feel safe in the world again.

You may think that your inner child is searching for a Twin Flame or a Guru or is wishing that she could go back in time to make her parents perfect parents. But this is simply not true.

What I have discovered is that all that your inner child is searching for, is **you**.

You are the parental self, and you are the child self and this is connected to the Holy Trinity, the Divine Mother within, the Divine Father within and the Divine Christ /Sophia child.

You are that eternal child and all you have ever been searching for and praying for, is your divine adult self.

Twin Flames and The Event Workbook
Working with your Inner Child Exercise

I would like to now share with you some powerful exercises that will enable you to connect very deeply to your child self.

Please take a pen and paper and write out all of the things that you loved to do as a child. Did you love drawing, painting, climbing, doing Lego, playing with dolls, writing or playing at being a teacher? Please take a moment to list all of the things that you loved to do as a child. When you have completed that list, which I would like you to add to often, please make a promise to yourself that you will start doing some of these activities again.

Twin Flames and The Event Workbook
Preview Chapter - The Power of Gratitude
"Gratitude is Vitamin for the Soul." Emmanuel Dagher

I cannot think of a more potent way to continue this workbook other than sharing a chapter on the power, the importance and the significance of gratitude on our spiritual path.

As mentioned over and over in my book, Twin flames and the Event, in order for us to obtain the levels of happiness and alignment that we are all deeply seeking, we must commit to a spiritual practice that enables us to guide and steer our consciousness towards that which is positive and uplifting.

If we do not have a spiritual practice, we will be swept along by the egoic consciousness, the egoic narrative, which is eternally committed to the false idea that you are separate, you have been abandoned and you do not belong in the universe.

Therefore, it is so important that we diligently commit for the rest of our lives to becoming obsessed with gratitude and subsequently going on rampages of gratitude.

Whenever we remember our day, may we all remember to reel off all of the things that we are grateful for.

This one spiritual act will shift your vibration and if you commit diligently to this practice, everyone around you will notice that your vibration has shifted.

When we commit to a spiritual practice of gratitude, we align our vibratory frequency with the benevolent force of creation.

We quickly realise that all of nature exists on a particular frequency band, and it is our duty as individualised transmitters of frequencies, to adjust our vibration in order to align with the benevolent force of creation - the sacred force that keeps all the stars in their place and turns a sperm and an egg into a baby.\

Essentially, we are all radio transmitters, and we are continuously absorbing thought forms from the matrix. These thought-forms very often are not personal to us, we are simply absorbing the collectives thought-forms.

Therefore, it is so important that we commit to the spiritual practice of becoming obsessed with being grateful, as in this way, we take governance over our egoic consciousness as opposed to allowing it to be hijacked by the negative matrix collective.

Twin Flames and The Event Workbook
Gratitude Exercise

I would like you to use the next two pages in this workbook, to write out in-depth all the things that you truly are grateful for.

I would like you to go into as much detail as possible. For example, if you are speaking about your parents and how grateful you are for them, please list all the reasons why you are grateful. Are you grateful for your mother's kindness? For her unconditional love? For the way she makes you laugh. Go into great detail about that which you are grateful for.

I would highly recommend putting on your list what you are grateful for - your body, about the fact that you have eyes to see, ears to hear, fingers to touch. Your loved ones. Really go into detail about all the things that you are grateful for.

If you are really committed to shifting your vibration, then you will take very seriously this exercise.

I highly recommend that you do this written exercise for 7 days (ideally using another journal), and if you are really committed to stabilising in the 5th dimension of consciousness, make a commitment to doing this exercise regularly for the rest of your life.

Please go on endless rampages of gratitude whenever you remember throughout your day. When you're washing up, when you're driving to collect the children, when you're going on a jog. I highly recommend becoming obsessed with gratitude. This is one of the most pertinent ways for you to shift your spiritual vibration permanently.

Commit deeply now in this moment to the path of gratitude.

If you do this today, it will mark the true beginning of the rest of your life.

Please use the notebook to write out all of the miracles and synchronicities you experience from doing this exercise and meditation.

To Purchase the Twin Flames and the Event Workbook, please visit this link:

<u>Twin Flames and The Event Workbook</u>

QR Codes to scan to access all of Jens Sacred Offerings are available at the back of this book.

Twin Flame and The Event Workbook
MP3 Activations

- Angel Wings

- Heart Space

- Hieros Gamos

- Inner Child Connection

- Law of Attraction

- Pineal Gland

- Stabilise in 5D

- Re-wilding

- Self-Love

- The Event

- Zero-Point

To Purchase the Twin Flames and the Event MP3 Activations, please visit this link:

Twin Flames and The Event Workbook and MP3 Activations

LAW OF ATTRACTION
LITTLE INSTRUCTION BOOK

I would like to share with you all now an excerpt from one of the most powerful books I've ever read, which happens to be a book that I created in 2011. It is my go-to book if I ever have a wobble which is very rare since 2013 but it is filled with so many codes that will immediately bring you back to stability in higher consciousness. The book consists of an introduction whereby I share with you all my downloads about how to work very deeply and powerfully with the law of attraction and the rest of the book is a combination of quotes and affirmations from well-known people that have worked successfully with the law of attraction.

Law of Attraction – Little Instruction Book
Preview Chapter

This is a book of miracles, a tale of timeless truth and a promise to the most ancient part of ourselves to remember and align with the highest vibration of who we are.

This is your eternal self-knocking at your door. There are gifts and promises encoded in these pages that will, if you allow them, unlock the timeless wisdom you carry within you.

We are all master creators, and we create everything we see and experience in our physical reality from the predominant thoughts and feelings we send out. We are vibrational beings, much like a radio transmitter; whatever we experience as our reality, is a direct reflection of the frequencies we emit.

We all possess innate powers to manifest the health, wealth, relationships and careers we desire and the fastest way to actualise this, is through a dedicated and regular practice of Gratitude.

Here is a sample of some of the quotes that are featured in the book:

"If you wish to find the secrets of the universe, think of energy, frequency and vibration."

~ Nikola Tesla

"Einstein proved that everything in the universe is energy. All energy vibrates at particular frequencies. We are energy too and so each of us is also vibrating at a frequency. Your thoughts, feelings and beliefs determine the vibration and frequency of your energy."

~ Rhonda Byrne

"There is no matter as such. All matter originates and exists only by virtue of a force which brings the particles of an atom to a vibration and holds this most minute solar system of the atom together. We must assume that behind this force is the existence of a conscious and intelligent mind. This mind is the matrix of all matter."

~ Max Planck

To Purchase the Law of Attraction – Little Instruction Book, please visit this link:

Law of Attraction - Little Instruction Book on Amazon

JENS SACRED OFFERINGS

Jen is very excited to be branching out with her spiritual work in order to share the original and powerful healing modalities that her higher self has shared with her.

MONTHLY GLOBAL TRANSMISSIONS

Since 2016 Jen has been hosting regular global transmissions on numerological portal dates such as 2:2, 3:3, 4:4 etc. Also, on Pagan holidays such as Samhain Imbolc, Equinox and Solstice. The reason for this is that it is so important that the Awakened Star Crew gather together on powerful dates such as these, in order to align our will and intention, with the will and intention of Mother Father God.

The ceremonies are a huge part of Jen's mission and she would love all of you reading these words to come and join her amazing Ground Crew Community who show up to take part in these ceremonies regularly.

Visit: http://www.jenmccarty.co.uk/

Many people report an immediate up-levelling in their spiritual vibration, through taking part in the global transmissions and this is due to the potency of gathering with hundreds of people and aligning our intentions with the intentions of our creator.

Most people experience massive shifts, particularly with regards to what is keeping them stuck at a lower vibrational level.

After and sometimes during these Transmissions people can get very emotional and can start crying due to clearing the energies and emotions that no longer serve them. This is a process of bringing the emotions to the surface and then releasing them, and it is always very important to trust that the process is happening in accordance with your Higher Self.

Most people find themselves listening to the Transmissions more than once because each time they listen to it, they find it continues to raise their vibration even higher and assist with shifting more toxic emotions.

Every day, Jen receives hundreds of messages and emails from people from all over the world, thanking her for her profound service to humanity.

Here is an example of the feedback Jen receives on a regular basis after hosting one of her large global ceremonies:

"Hi Jen, I loved last night's ceremony. Just wanted to say all your ceremonies have literally raised my kundalini. I have flashes, cracks, rushes and full-blown activations every time... just wanted to say as it is so special to me and it is an affirmation for you that you are working your powerful magic... Blessings, protection and loads of love to you xxx"

"I have just done the ceremony on replay.... WOW!!! It was amazing, lots of kundalini shaking and shivering.... thank you Jen' **KS**

"The transmission was so powerful and beautiful! Thank you so much Jen! I am still new to follow you and your work, so this was only my second opportunity to participate in one of your transmissions. I really felt the cleansing, healing and support of Archangel Michael and Saint Germain."

"For years I've had pain between my shoulder blades and last night I finally felt it released and surrendered. I felt such pure, unconditional love and once we came to unite in the light with our Divine counterparts, my face was filled with a huge smile and tears were just rolling and flowing out of me to cleanse and purify. I felt pure light and love emanating throughout my whole being. - JV"

"Jen, it was one of the greatest experiences I've ever had in meditation—truly powerful portals of 5D opened up and shifted this realm profoundly. So grateful! And I feel so blessed to participate with you live. Just spectacular! Sending you angel kisses - KK"

Visit: http://www.jenmccarty.co.uk/

MARY MAGDALENE FEAST DAY CEREMONY
JULY 2021 GLOBAL TRANSMISSION

Twin Soul Ascension Report
All 144,000 Twin Souls Must Unite Now

This book was written between two very important portal dates – Summer Solstice 2021 and Mary Magdalene Feast Day 21st of July 2021 and therefore I have included the Twin Soul Ascension Report which I also wrote in that potent time period.

Dearest brothers and sisters,

Greetings of the most high. We come forward now, in this moment of your time with much news to share with you ever-evolving humanity.

I would like to take this opportunity to remind everyone that abiding peace can only be sourced in the present moment. It is very important that everyone reading these words find a spiritual practice to anchor to at these profoundly transformative times that we are going through as a collective.

The spiritual practices I recommend and advocate are: resting as awareness for short moments and going on endless rampages of gratitude.

Whenever we commit to a spiritual practice, we send subconscious messages to our egoic victim narrative, that it is no longer in the driving seat of our consciousness.

We are communicating to it that our higher self is beginning to take over the reins. I really cannot express how important it is, brothers and sisters, for you to take heed of these words. It is very important that you are stabilized at this time of great planetary shift.

There are so many people around you who are relying on you to be truly anchored in present moment consciousness, the zero point field to assist them to navigate these unprecedented times.

It's very important that everyone reading these words understand that the despicable powers that "were" are truly scraping the bottom of the barrow now in order to try to create division and separation in humanity.

It is always advisable to use critical thinking at all times when it comes to the issues and agendas, particularly anything perpetuated by the mainstream media.

You have to apply critical thinking and think to yourself, who is this agenda benefiting? Is it giving more control and power to the de-letes? Or is it empowering humanity?

You will find that most of the agendas that are being exposed at the moment have been orchestrated to harness and collect more power for the powers that were and disempower humanity.

Therefore, please do not give your time or energy to any mainstream media agendas. This is very, very important. Particularly if you are an awakened star seed, it is absolutely fundamental that you do not feed these divisive controlled narratives that have been deeply designed to orchestrate separation and profound division in our beautiful society.

It is best to focus on your own inner world, go on rampages of kindness, remembering that every single one of your brothers and sisters is suffering from PTSD to some degree from being incarnated into the matrix, which has sought to degrade and deny every single one of God's children's divinity and innate sacredness.

It has been very challenging for all of us to be incarnated into the matrix. And one of the most profound ways to shift your vibration permanently is to approach all your brothers and sisters with deep love, compassion, kindness, and understanding that everyone is suffering on some level to some degree on the spectrum of trauma.

The energies are now building up towards the Magdalene feast day and the day out of time, it is only recently that the Catholic church has acknowledged Mary Magdalene as a Saint and has awarded her a feast day.

It is very important that we, the awakened ground crew, come together to celebrate this feast day and acknowledge the role of the divine feminine in terms of harnessing the new earth energies into the collective.

In this transmission, we will be activating the Magdalene flame that resides within all. Everyone is born with a spark /potential to realize their eternal divinity.

We will be working with many powerful energies, which will transform the spark of the Magdalene flame to become a fully fledged roaring fire indicative of she who burns as one who walks as the Magdalene.

This is appropriate for men and women as the divine feminine energies reside both in men and women as do the divine masculine energies reside within both men and women.

In the Magdalene transmission, we will also be working to activate galactic intervention for this current 3D con-vid narrative. And we will be working with the higher self of all of the military and police offices to put down their helmets and join humanity and protect us.

Please know it is my deepest honor to serve you all, my brothers and sisters. And I will continue to show up with the transmissions and continue to show up with these ascension reports. In this transmission we will work deeply with the energies of the Divine feminine Christ known as Sophia also known as Magdalene.

We will all receive a powerful light language dispensation that will enable us to become full embodiments of the Magdalene. Magdalene is the rebel she is unafraid to walk alone and she will stand in her truth in protection of the vulnerable, regardless of anyone's opinion of her.

It is very important that we empower this flame of sovereignty and Divine femininity in as many brothers and sisters as possible.

In this transmission we will also be working with the higher self of all police officers and military to communicate to them on a spiritual soul consciousness level to put down their helmets and join humanity as we take our planet back from the dark despicable powers that have hijacked our planet for eons.

It is very important that the ground crew come forward to participate in this global ceremony as the more of us who gather on our grid points, the quicker we will activate the shift in the Collective..........

This is extremely important work for the collective and for all our future generations to come, and we have an extremely powerful and solid ground crew who are deeply committed to showing up continuously for this global ceremonial work. **In love and eternal light Jenji and the White Wolf tribe.**

To receive monthly Twin Soul Ascension Reports, please sign-up for Jens free E-Newsletter:

<u>Twin Soul Ascension Reports E-Newsletter</u>

MP3 ACTIVATION SERIES

In addition to the global transmissions, Jen has been guided by spirit to produce specific transmissions which address certain topics affecting the collective consciousness. This makes it much easier for people to be able to choose which area of their life they wish to work on to address their personal challenges. For example, reclaiming your self-worth and healing sexual trauma etc.

These activations attune you specifically to fifth dimensional consciousness – the feedback and results so far have been truly mind-blowing, with many people reporting crying the deepest tears they have ever known, and many people have said they were miraculously contacted by their Twin Flame around the time of completing these activations.

Here is a list of activations which are available to download in MP3 format at time of press;

- Abundance

- Age Regeneration

- Angelic T-Cell

- Atlantis Timeline

- Love your physical body

- Catalyst Twin Clearing

- Deep Relaxation

- Earth Star Chakra

- Inner Child Healing

- Light Language Dispensation

- Meet the 5D Aspect of your Twin Flame

- Miracle IBS Healing

- Spiritual Protection

- Rebalance giving with receiving

- Relaxation

- Reviving the Frozen Garden of your Heart

- Self-Worth

- Shame and Guilt Clearing

- Source Frequency

- St Germain

- Violet Waterfall

- Yeshua & Magdalene Divine Union

- Yoni Nidra

- Zero Point Activation

To Purchase the MP3 Activation Series, please visit this link:

MP3 Activation Series

QR Codes to scan to access all of Jens Sacred Offerings are available at the back of this book.

SPECIAL MP3 ACTIVATIONS

I also have two special activations; one is called the "Yoni Nidra" and the other is called "Miracle IBS Healing". These are long in-depth healing meditations, that will massively affect your healing journey and spiritual vibration.

YONI NIDRA

The Yoni Nidra MP3 is a powerful visualisation exercise that will enable you to connect deeply with your Yoni (vagina) if you are a divine feminine.

There are very powerful and potent codes within this visualisation which will assist you to shift huge amounts of trauma and abuse personally and collectively that you may have stored within your womb area.

Many people report having miraculous healings with their sexuality, for example having a much-heightened orgasmic potential. It has also helped many beloved's come into union with their next soul partner.

I really highly recommend working with the Yoni Nidra mp3.

MIRACLE IBS HEALING

In this powerful MP3 you will be guided on a very deep journey to the Australian bush to meet all the aboriginal elders who are guardians of your deepest sense of belonging in the universe. So much of the discomfort that we experience in our bodies derive from the core belief that we are unsafe, and we don't belong in this world.

This is an extremely powerful miraculous life-changing MP3 that will guide you on a memorable journey deep into the Australian bush to meet elders of your soul tribe, that will re-establish your position within the tribe in order to help you heal the deepest core emotional traumas that you are carrying particularly around feeling safe in the world and belonging. This MP3 is extremely effective for anyone who is suffering from stomach problems such as Crohn's disease or IBS.

21 DAY ACTIVATION PROGRAMS

I am so excited to be sharing this powerful and sacred work with my community. There are lots of different ways in which you can work with me; in my containers, in my facilitator trainings and with my MP3 activation programs.

Each 21-day activation program comes with a meditation which is highly activating for your DNA plus an E-Book with exercises to follow during the 21 days.

It is highly advisable to work with a program for 21 days as it gives you enough time to take on a brand-new habit and it is our habits that ultimately change our life.. I have been getting the most phenomenal feedback from all the people in my community that have been doing these programs and they are highly advisable if you wish to pass chat your spiritual evolution.

Please visit the 21 Day Program Menu at:
http://www.jenmccarty.co.uk/

ATTRACT 1 MILLION FOLLOWERS

Transform your relationship with social media and become an influencer in record time.

Something really amazing happened to me! I spontaneously went into a very deep meditation and my spirit guides took me on a journey and they showed me incredibly powerful symbols, totems and guides that are specifically connected to increasing the amount of followers and subscribers that you have on social media.

My guides took me on a journey, and it was absolutely awe inspiring. On that journey I encountered many souls who are in the 5th Dimensional millionaire mindset. They were high vibing souls that were holding space for us all in the higher realms as we up-level our spiritual vibration and massively up-level and increase the number of followers we have.

So therefore, I am absolutely delighted to inform all of you that I have channelled and created a meditation whereby you program your subconscious mind in an extremely powerful and proficient way to attract a huge number of followers. It is so important in these transformational times that the souls that have attracted huge followings be aligned with God consciousness.

It is really important that we on the spiritual path have an engaged and high-level following so that we can share our inspiration and deep insights with as many people as possible in order to activate their DNA so that they can awaken.

There is a very, very deep reason why we would have that desire to have a large following and it is not because we just want people to like our cheek bones and silly selfies – it is not about that at all!

It is about the frequency and the vibration – getting our frequency and vibration out there to as many people as possible in order to help them awaken out of the spell of the matrix.

This meditation program is extremely powerful and will transform your spiritual vibration on a very deep and lasting level. Please understand that this progam is not simply just a meditation. There is a PDF E-Book that goes with this meditation which gives practical guidance on how to transform your vibration and become magnetic to the followers that you have made a soul contract to inspire in this lifetime.

I will share with you, life-changing habits that will massively affect your vibration very, very quickly. It is very important that everyone commits to practice this meditation program for 21 days.

To Purchase the Attract 1 Million Followers Program, please visit this link:

Attract 1 Million Followers Program

QR Codes to scan to access all of Jens Sacred Offerings are available at the back of this book.

MIRACLE HAIR GROWTH

I would like to share with you all the reason why I was inspired to create this miracle hair growth meditation program.

I was recently hanging out with a good friend of mine and she told me that she had a friend who had alopecia and she had a clear dream that her hair grew back, and the first aspect of her hair follicles that started to grow back were her eyelashes. The dream was so vivid that she was inspired to go and buy her a hairbrush, she then went to her place of work and bought her a hairbrush and told her that her hair is growing.

She waited for 4 weeks and she heard back from the woman who said that indeed her eyelashes did indeed grow back and now her hair was growing.

This story showed me and proved to me the power of our individual consciousness to activate miracles in our personal realities and this story inspired me to create this meditation program as this is absolute proof that miracles are possible in the area of hair growth.

I hope and pray that you take inspiration from this story and know that anything is possible.

Upon hearing the story, I was inspired to do some exploring in the Akashik records and I discovered that this issue was specifically targeted at the time of the fall of Atlantis, as the nefarious powers that took over the power that men held on a spiritual level and they sought to eradicate that and control that through gene manipulation. Specifically targeting the hair growth follicles in the male collective psyche.

Please know that this has now been corrected and each of us who do this meditation deeply empowers this brand-new healed and whole timeline for all the future generations to come.

To Purchase the Miracle Hair Growth Program, please visit this link:

<u>Miracle Hair Growth Program</u>

QR Codes to scan to access all of Jens Sacred Offerings are available at the back of this book.

EMF PROTECTION

There are no words that can adequately express how powerful we all are.

One of the main things that has been targeted with humanity is their connection to the individual power source - their own DNA.

This was controlled and manipulated at the time of Atlantis and a huge disempowerment codon was activated within our perfected 12 strand DNA patterning which was scrambled to become a two stranded DNA configuration.

We as the enlightened ground-crew have been ordained with the spiritual task of re-correcting the distortions that took place at the time of Atlantis.

We each have the power to be able to communicate with our DNA to tell it to oscillate at a level whereby it is no longer affected by EMF warfare radiation.

However, until we get to the level of absolute unequivocal faith, I do recommend working with external devices such as Shungite, Black tourmaline and Tesla frequency devices such as the Healy machine.

This meditation progam is extremely powerful and life changing and will assist you massively to be completely invulnerable to EMF radiation

To Purchase the EMF Protection Program, please visit this link:

EMF Protection Program

QR Codes to scan to access all of Jens Sacred Offerings are available at the back of this book.

ABUNDANCE – TRANSFORM YOUR WEALTH BLUEPRINT

I have experienced breakthrough after breakthrough since I looked at my wealth blueprint and realised that it had stagnated. This meditation program which I have brought through is very powerful and will work on a deep energetic level to transform your relationship with wealth and abundance.

The program assists you to align with all of the riches of the Kingdom and Queendom of Mother-Father-God and transform your wealth blueprint forever.

AGE REGENERATION

One of the first things I realised when I had my powerful spiritual awakening when I was 21, was that Mother-Father-God in all her infinite brilliance created these vessels for our souls to co-exist in for as long as we choose.

In my Awakening, I understood deeply that the aging agenda was a program that was implemented at a certain time within our planetary history to control and prevent us from living up to 1,000 - 2,000 years as per our original blueprint as designed by Mother-Father-God.

Follow this 21 Day Program to really deeply communicate to your unconscious mind and fully align on the timeline whereby you can experience the regeneration of all of your aging codons in your DNA.

DIVINE LOVE

This program will enable you to become extremely magnetic to your true divine counterpart.

Commit to this 21 Day program and observe the shifts and transformation to your magnetism as you up-level your value in your self-worth and become truly magnetic to your divine love.

You will notice the difference in your spiritual vibration and will be able to sit back and observe the change as you become more magnetic to your spiritual destiny.

I highly recommend this program to everyone who is drawn to work with me there are codes and symbols that are shared in the meditation that completely bypassed the conscious rational mind and inform the unconscious mind that you truly are ready to step into your divine union right now.

BECOME A CERTIFIED QUANTUM TIME TRAVEL TECHNIQUE PRACTITIONER

Practitioner Levels I & II

The Quantum Time Travel Technique (QTTT) is a technique that Jen has brought through, that she used in many of her 1-2-1 sessions.

This is a paradigm shifting tool that can effortlessly slip into your healing practice to ensure once and for all that all major deep core issues are cleared entirely from you and your client's field forever!

Jen's intention with this powerful Ascension training is to provide people with the ability to offer 1-2-1 healing sessions with their clients.

QTTT will work alongside many healing modalities such as Reiki, Acupuncture, Theta Healing, Womb Work, Sexuality Healing and any other spiritual alignment work.

Jen is very keen to bring QTTT to the world, as it will bring so much healing which is greatly needed at the moment. Earth is going through so many shifts currently and so many people are healing from deep unprocessed trauma particularly from their childhood.

QTTT is an accelerated healing modality that has been brought forth in order to deeply support the collective in clearing huge quantities of traumatised and stuck energy.

The Quantum Time Travel Technique teaches:

▶ The basic principles of counselling a client in a session

▶ How to hold space for a client - what this means and what this entails

▶ Take your client on a healing journey – taking their future self to meet their past traumatised and frozen self

▶ How to identify and release core trauma

▶ Completely set the child-self free

▶ Enable emotional healing to take place, so that the clients growth trajectory may begin

Join live trainings facilitated by Jen via online webinars. In these training sessions there are plenty of opportunities to practice on fellow students, ensuring that they come away feeling positive and confident with regards to facilitating their own healing sessions.

All Certified QTTT Practitioners have not only found they have benefited from the amazing healing benefits of this technique but also experienced the most amazing feedback on the healing benefits received by their clients.

Below is some of the latest feedback which Jen received following the graduation ceremony recently held for her first training of QTTT Level 1 in November 2020:

"I have been through a lot of serious trauma in my life and worked on this for many years in different ways. I have also trained to guide others and help them deal with their own issues. Up until QTTT I had never experienced a way of doing things that really integrated the past traumatised self, that part that was blocked and stuck and how to bring the whole me back together! The times for endless psychotherapy and endlessly going round in circles is long, long gone. Those ways don't help most people, they just keep the old pain going. I felt called to start my practise again, as I know that when the truth of these times comes out (disclosure) there will be a lot of people needing help. Something was holding me back, Spirit said wait, so I waited and then came QTTT!"

The QTTT training ran for the first time in October 2020 and will run again in 2021 and will be facilitated via live webinar sessions over a six-week period. Jen already has a waiting list of people who have benefitted from this amazing healing modality and are eager to learn the technique for themselves, either to serve as an additional therapy to integrate into their current healing work or for those who wish to learn the technique, so that they may use it on their friends and family.

Since QTTT Level 1 Practitioner Training was such an amazing success – Jen decided to develop Level II which explores QTTT at a much deeper level. In QTTT II we will be accessing a much deeper exploration into alternative modalities that can be used with this technique, such as working with one's future self - working with the spirit of ancestors that have passed and working with the spirit of one's Twin Flame. Including working with totems ascended masters and archangels. Most if not all candidates who have completed Level I, have already signed up for the pre-book list for Level II.

To learn more about the Quantum Time Travel Technique and find out more about training to become a QTTT Certified Practitioner visit:

QTTT Practitioner Training

QUANTUM WEALTH MASTERMIND

Jen has been working with the most incredible mentors who are anchored in millionaire mindset, and has now shifted a lot of her work to sharing about millionaire mindset and wealth coaching. She is offering regular live training throughout the year as well as many self-paced programs. These trainings and programs are packed with Ascension codes that will enable you to up level your spiritual vibration very quickly and very efficiently.

Jen is an extremely powerful facilitator and it is highly recommended to sign up to the live trainings whereby you get close access to Jen. If you are unable to attend the live trainings then we highly recommend working with the self-paced programs. Jen is continuously bringing through powerful life changing programs that will massively affect your spiritual vibration and enable you to stabilise in unity consciousness.

To learn more about the Wealth Mastermind Live and Self-Paced Trainings, please visit:

Wealth Mastermind Live / Self-Paced Trainings

Jen has brought through a 5D Business Program which can also be found on her website.

4 WEEK SPIRITUAL MASTERY PROGRAM

This is one of the most powerful offerings that Jen has brought through and every person that has done the course has gone on to fully stabilize in fifth dimensional consciousness, and has become a teacher, leader, and wayshower - building their own Communities and becoming a role model within them.

This is an extremely powerful course whereby Jen literally holds your hand and walks you into 5th Dimensional consciousness. Sharing with you, all of the tools and techniques and practices that she used to be fully stabilised in 5th dimensional consciousness since October 2013.

This course has been created to assist you on an exceptionally deep level, to align vibrationally with the frequencies of fifth dimensional consciousness. This is an extremely powerful offering that has been brought through in divine timing, to assist those of you who identify as Twin Flame Starseeds. You will be given powerful tools which will assist you to rise up as the illuminated beacon that you have come here to be.

The course comes in four parts. Each part will include a darshan (which is a sacred discourse on the week's subject matter), a powerful visualisation (to assist you to crucially clear many old false beliefs) and the course most importantly includes homework for you to carry out each week, which will train you to formulate new patterns and habits that are in alignment with fifth dimensional consciousness.

The whole purpose of the course is to educate you and remind you, that in order to fully stabilise in higher dimensional consciousness, it is absolutely imperative that you are empowered to take actions every single day that are in alignment with fifth dimensional consciousness.

I invite you to open your heart and open your palms to receive this guidance, as for many of you, this is what your higher selves are very much wanting to deliver to you at this particular conjecture on your evolutionary cycle. And for many of you, you will find that following through with the teachings of this course, will be the answer to your deepest prayers.

It is time now for those who promised to be the illuminated ones, the enlightened ones and the way-showers to step forward now, embodying their full spiritual mastery.

Please visit: <u>4 Week Spiritual Mastery Course</u>

4 Week Spiritual Mastery Program Testimonial

"This is my testimony of how POWERFUL Jen McCarty's four-week spiritual mastery course is!

Since receiving just before Xmas, I have to say the "jewels' ' of self-mastery information are amazing and if you know anything about this Twin Flame journey, you will know that full self-mastery and self-love is what brings you into union.

I'm on my 2nd time listening to it and putting the homework into practice. I have to say my connection to Self and Source is so much stronger. I am always seeing 33, 44, 55, 222, 333, 444, 555 and 144. I am grounding myself into the present moment a lot more, BELIEVING in the power of my imagination and so much more.

"I don't want to give too much away. I just want to say to anyone who is genuinely needing help on their spiritual path, this four-week course is the key and is worth every penny."

I have to be honest I always wanted to buy the course, but my financial situation would not have allowed me to for now. Obviously, Source knew I needed this and it would propel me into alignment, and I actually won the course, little old me who never wins anything. Talk about Divine intervention and timing lol.

But again, I can't stress enough how amazing this course is, thank you Jen McCarty, you are doing such amazing work, may God continue to bless you."

TESLA TECHNOLOGY
HEALY MACHINE

The Healy is a bio-resonance tool that works to support your body's energetic field and promote deep cellular healing.

The Healy is a small, very complex piece of equipment. Using precise frequencies and low intensity currents, the Healy works to reverse the process of decreasing cell voltage by restoring the natural voltage of the cell membrane.

Compromised cells lead us to experience a debilitating range of different symptoms, such as the inability to concentrate, learning difficulties, stress/burnout, physical diseases and illness, slow recovery from injury, cellulite, skin breakouts, mental health challenges and emotional instability.

Recently I was very privileged to be invited to be part of the team that has bought through the Healy devise. This is incredible Tesla Technology that works with the principle of vibrational frequencies.

A few days ago, my friend reached out to me and asked me if I had heard of the Healy machine and she told me that she was diagnosed as being in full-blown menopause, she had had blood tests and a full doctor's analysis which confirmed that she is in full-blown menopause.

She had one session whereby the practitioner sent her some specific resonances for hormones and after having no period for a long time, her period came back in less than five days.

I was really blown away when I heard this, and it touched something deep inside of me to go and explore what is the Healy.

I was then led to the Healy testimony page and I have no words that can adequately express how blown away I am by the testimonies....

As you may know I have not got behind any products since I launched my offerings to the world and that is because I've never found a product that I 100% resonate with, but I know that I found this with the Healy.

Based on the testimonies that I read I decided to go ahead and buy the Healy.

There seems to be a huge buzz in the UK with lots and lots of people being ready to purchase and jump on board the Healy train...

It is such a phenomenal investment on all levels spiritually, physically and financially I made my money back within 24 hours of purchasing the machine and they even sent me a brand-new Healy machine which I have given to my assistant.

Here is a link to all products:

<u>Healy Products</u>

Healy Testimonials

I will now include some testimonies from the feedback page and the link to the feedback page...

<u>Healy Facebook Group</u>

I honestly thought Healy was something I'd try and send back as I was very skeptical. I'm only on day 12 of using it and I'm off my daily antihistamines for hay fever and miraculously I am sleeping all night without 2 sleeping pills that I have been on for over 10 years!!! If I ever went without them, I would lie wide awake all night having hot and cold sweats. I am gob smacked! I don't understand HOW it works but it DOES work.

Still waiting for my Healy but my girlfriend is doing distant healing which I have benefited from immensely. An incredible pain left in an incredible 3 mins flat.

So, the other day I was in so much pain and my friend ran the pain program for me. He is in NC and I am in AZ. I could feel warmth flooding the area. It was so healing, I fell asleep, and the pain was gone.

Increasing my energy and confidence and decreasing pain after years of chronic fatigue

In answer to the question what do you love most about your Healy? That it can help so many people and animals, with health, vitality and overall, well-being!

Or I place them on positive words while vibrating matching frequencies. For this I'm mainly placing them on the words. "Self-love and acceptance" As a Time-Waver practitioner has made me a program for this.

Final words: I've been very impressed with the level of support that I have received in terms of learning how to use the device and also how to operate the back office when it comes to signing up new members.

For all of you who are ready to jump on board now and make the most of this offer that is going to end as soon as possible here is the link for you to buy the Healy machine....

Please email me at cosmicgypsy33@gmail.com to receive more information on the Healy machine attentively please click this link;

https://www.healyworld.net/en/the-product-world/

If you are wanting to purchase a Healy machine, please use the link below with my name, this means that you will be added onto my team and will most likely receive a huge amount of commission.

https://partner.healyworld.net/jenmccarty144

https://www.jenmccarty.co.uk/healy-machine

ABOUT THE AUTHOR

Jen McCarty

Widely known as the Healer of the Healers - Jen McCarty has earned the most astonishing place in everyone's heart. Jen assists people with addiction recovery, as well as helping many people heal their core wounds on a soul level. Jen had a massive life-changing Kundalini Awakening when she was just 21, in the Himalayas in Northern India, chanting the mantra "Om Namah Shivaya". From that moment on she passed over the threshold from third dimension Consciousness to stabilising in fifth Dimensional Consciousness.

Jen has since devoted her whole adult life serving her Brothers and Sisters and has been blessed with a massive amount of extremely dedicated followers over the last 5 years and has built up a social media following of over 175,000 people.

Jen specialises in working with the reunion of Twin Flames and the removal of roadblocks that stand in the way of that. She is an awakened spiritual teacher, deeply and highly skilled at facilitating a space for all those who she comes into contact with. She has a phenomenal track record in uniting many, many Twin Flames, assisting them to connect with their Multi-Dimensional aspect and activating the Hieros Gamos – the inner alchemical marriage of the masculine and feminine energies within, and very skillfully identifying and removing all blocks that stand in the way of triumphant Twin Flame Union.

Jen has been working quite specifically with the Twin Flame Community and her skills are vast and varied – she can help bring in greater levels of abundance, greater health, well-being, weight-loss and also assists people to align with their soul's highest density.

Jen has earned access to the Akashic Records through the purification of her own heart, through her own personal Ascension process. This enables her to bring forth potent wisdom, in order to assist you in successfully completing the lessons you incarnated to master.

Jen has facilitated a number of global spiritual retreats – which were hosted recently at Glastonbury and Mount Shasta.

Many consider working with Jen McCarty truly the fast track to spiritual awakening and Twin Flame reunion. The results of Jen's work so far have been truly mind-blowing, her monthly global transmissions are regularly attended by 800+ fellow spiritual seekers and many people say that she has become one of the world's leading change makers in the spiritual community, assisting her beloved Brothers and Sisters discover the harmony and alignment with God Consciousness, that they have been perpetually seeking.

Many of Jen's community feel absolutely blessed and fortunate to have the opportunity to connect with Jen in a personal setting. Since Jen's community has gone from strength to strength, she is unable to spend time counselling individual clients due to the waiting lists becoming too long.

Jen has experienced huge breakthroughs recently due to working with very high-level mentors who are fully anchored in millionaire mindset. This is having a huge impact on her working and her offerings that she has begun to share. Please check out her website for information on transforming your wealth blueprint.

Jen wants to be able to assist as many people as possible and therefore her membership community was born to serve the collective, as opposed to using up all her energy on individual sessions.

JOIN JEN'S SACRED COMMUNITIES ON SOCIAL MEDIA

Linktree - cosmicgypsy33

Instagram - Official Jen McCarty

Facebook - Jen McCarty23 Personal Profile

Facebook Group - The Event is Happening

YouTube - Cosmic Gypsy

Telegram Group - The Event is Happening

Gab - JenJen144

MeWe - JenMcCarty2

Twitter - Jen McCarty

BOOK IMAGE ARTIST: Emily Irena Kenyon

Emily is divinely creative in all ways, being a natural and intuitive artist, she can be given any idea or request and turn it into something truly beautiful. At age 12, she joined Instagram and discovered the world of animal photography and went to her mum and gleefully proclaimed "That's what I want to do! I want to do what they do!!" Luckily her mum was a photographer and promptly bought her a camera and got started teaching her all about photography. At age

13 years Emily attended college and completed a Level 1 and Level 3 Diploma in Photography. When she paints she goes into a zone which 'simply does', and honouring herself, the Divine feminine and our truly magical, powerful, explosive, beautiful, yet vulnerable predicament as loving light beings on earth at this time. In her paintings she transmits all this energy into whatever she paints and clients are often blown away by her work.

You can find her work here @emilysartcompany on both Facebook and Instagram.

QR Codes

Please scan the following QR Codes for access to Jen's sacred offerings.

Books / Workbooks and Audiobooks

No More Crumbs Workbook

No More Crumbs Audiobook

Twin Flames and The Event Book on Amazon

Twin Flames and The Event Workbook and MP3 Activations

Twin Flames and The Event Audiobook on Amazon

Law of Attraction - Little Instruction Book on Amazon

JENS SACRED OFFERINGS

Monthly Global Transmissions

MP3 Activation Series

21 DAY ACTIVATION PROGRAMS

Attract 1 Million Followers Program

Miracle Hair Growth Program

EMF Protection Program

LIVE TRAININGS AND SELF-PACED PROGRAMS

QTTT Practitioner Training

Wealth Mastermind Live / Self-Paced Trainings

4 Week Spiritual Mastery Course

JENS NEWSLETTER AND SOCIAL MEDIA CHANNELS

<u>Jens Monthly Twin Souls Ascension Report</u>

<u>Jens Personal Instagram Page</u>

<u>Jens Personal Facebook Page</u>

The Event is Happening Facebook Group

Jens YouTube Channel - Cosmic Gypsy

Telegram Group - The Event is Happening

Jens Gab Page

Jens Twitter Page

Made in the USA
Columbia, SC
09 November 2021